GETTING
Naked
AGAIN

GETTING *Naked* AGAIN

Dating,
Romance,
Sex, and Love
When You've Been
Divorced,
Widowed,
Dumped, or
Distracted

JUDITH SILLS, PhD

SPRINGBOARD

NEW YORK   BOSTON

Springboard Press
Hachette Book Group
237 Park Avenue, New York, NY 10017

Visit our Web site at www.HachetteBookGroup.com.
Springboard Press is an imprint of Grand Central Publishing.
The Springboard Press name and logo are trademarks of
Hachette Book Group, Inc.

First Edition: February 2009

Library of Congress Cataloging-in-Publication Data
Sills, Judith.
    Getting naked again : dating, romance, sex, and love when you've
been divorced, widowed, dumped, or distracted / Judith Sills.
      p. cm.
    ISBN-13: 978-0-446-58249-0
    1. Middle-aged women—Sexual behavior. 2. Baby boom
generation—Attitudes. 3. Dating (Social customs). 4. Love.
5. Single people—Psychology. I. Title.

HQ29.S55 2009
646.7'70844—dc22   2007048791

10 9 8 7 6 5 4 3 2 1

Book design by Charles Sutherland

Printed in the United States of America

CONTENTS

PART II
Interpersonal Expertise

GETTING
Naked
AGAIN

PART ONE

Personal Evolution

CHAPTER ONE

Reentry
or
Would I Sleep with Eisenhower?

*I*t was all very unlikely. She was standing in the hallway of the Marriott Marquis Hotel, wearing cute wrinkled Nick & Nora cotton pajamas, the white ones with the cherries printed on them and the small ruffles at the wrists and ankles. She was deciding whether to knock on the door of a friendly colleague who, earlier in the conference, had patted her calf in a suggestive manner but allowed her to retire to her hotel room alone. He had seemed interested, definitely interested, though he had done no more than extend an indirect invitation and wait to see if she would RSVP.

But she was fifty-six years old, and it was more than twenty-five years since she had responded to a calf rub offered by a man other than her now ex-husband. Still, that husband had been, for the last two years, rubbing someone else's considerably younger calf—and wasn't it ever going to be her turn again? That was the question that got her up, out of her hotel room, and into this awkward moment of indecision in a hotel hallway. Apparently, if it were ever to be her turn again, if she were ever going to kiss someone again, smile up at, hold hands with, not to mention the rest, well, something would be required of her. The new lover, new boyfriend, new companion, new man was not going to be delivered effortlessly into her life. At some point, she would have to knock.

So will you.

Because, however it happened, you're back out there floating in single space. Whether you have been cast back out by painful circumstance, or you are finally back after years of hiding out, at this moment you are romantically unattached and on your own. And, by whatever process that has brought you to this brink, you are considering a return to the game.

That game would be the timeworn, thrilling, and terrible drama of flirtation, sex, and love; of courtship and romance; of getta-guy, getta-girl, or get gotten. How consciously and there-fore how successfully you replay the game is the subject of this book. First you have to decide to knock.

You may be, at this moment in your life, very far from that hallway. Perhaps you are still frozen in the grip of a loss, stagger-ing after a death or a betrayal. And even if your recovery from these wounds has brought you as far as this door, you may still be paralyzed in its face. The sexual and emotional experience available across the threshold is still far outside your picture of yourself. But you are considering a move in that direction.

On the other hand, had it been a different version of you in the hallway, you might never have retreated to your room to think it over. You may be one of those who threw herself over that threshold and out of those damn pajamas twenty minutes after your last relationship ended. (Or, to be on the safe side, twenty minutes before.) You are trading partners, changing stories, and eager to avoid a hole in your heart or in your life. You have leapt headlong into courtship, perhaps without some of the strategies you'll need to make it turn out better this time.

Most of us are somewhere between these two positions—wishing to reconnect in some important way, longing to have a little fun or a lot of sex or a great companion, but anxious, discouraged, or cynical about the possibility of happily ever after. Much as we have not given up on the fantasy of romance, affection, and love, we are undone at the prospect of reengaging in the tiresome and hurtful dating game that carries with it these rewards. Eventually, though, most of us wrestle with the reality: It's the only game in town.

All of us who are single—whether widowed or divorced, dumped or thankfully detached, or just newly resurfaced after the distractions of motherhood, career, or both—stand at the same anxious precipice. Must I, will I get back into the game of courtship? Would I want to? Can I bear its rigors? Is it worth it? Am I still a contender? Can I do it any better this time? Or at all? And, since it definitely requires two to play, where do I go to find someone with whom to get up a game?

These are legitimate questions at any age, but they can be showstoppers after, say, forty-six. That's when we add the fretful salsa of age to our always conflicted feelings about dating. True, an amazing number of thirty-two-year-olds have been known to convince themselves that it is already too late. *Old* is not a belief confined to the "mature" woman or man. *Too late* is a destructive thought, whether at thirty-five or at eighty, but an awful lot of us over forty or fifty run it through our brains anyway.

For the moment, you are at your tennis club contemplating the decent-looking retiree across the dining room—single, sixty-eight, wearing whites and a knee brace—and you think, "Jeez, wouldn't that be like sleeping with Eisenhower?" It's a thought that could send you right off to babysit full-time for your own grandchildren, confining yourself to book groups and community service—all perfectly fine occupations if they are satisfying enough for you. But some of us stop to recall that, as it turned out, Eisenhower had someone on the side after Mamie apparently lost interest. We take another look across the dining room and see past the knee brace. We decide to knock.

Woman in Transition

Whether you are poised hesitantly at this brink or you've thrown yourself relentlessly, determinedly into the online, blind-date, hookup bars middle of the middle-aged dating world, you are at a life stage you might think of as *reentry*. Reentry is a tricky time, and it requires more preparation and self-awareness than merely how best to market yourself with a great computer profile. (Though such advice helps—no question about it.) If you are looking for a safe and happy landing, reentry needs some solid-state understanding of the process and a damn good heat shield.

That is the purpose of this book. For one reason or another, you unexpectedly find yourself in the untethered universe of single life. To move from that romantic free fall toward a loving connection, you will have to navigate an intensely emotional, uncertain, and unsettling period of time.

The internal forces that will drive you during this period—your own individual fears and longings, your lifelong romantic patterns, and your acute reentry needs—are powerful, unexpected, and erratic. It would help to have some meaningful self-knowledge to steer a safe course. Yet your capacity for introspection and self-awareness may well have atrophied during your marriage or motherhood, when you focused so much on taking care of other people that you lost close touch with yourself.

Now here you are, thrown back on that self you may no longer know well, negotiating your own mixed feelings while you are recovering from emotional loss. Just catching up with your inner life could be a full-time preoccupation. But many of us are tempted to skip this inner step entirely. The outer drama of e-mail flirtation, social competition, and actual foreplay can be so compelling, confusing, or aversive that we miss a clear picture of ourselves because we are too busy watching the show.

That show, the interpersonal soap opera of dating, will involve meeting, assessing, kissing, touching, wooing, and negotiating with some stranger. And his children. Plus his friends. Not to mention his ex-wife, past girlfriends, medical history, financial fetishes, sexual aspirations, political biases, and his odd habit of saving string and old *Playboy* magazines because he still believes the collection is valuable.

Anywhere along this rocky way you might dismiss him, which will exhaust and discourage you, even though you are the one to do the dumping. Or he might reject you—which will sting even if you had already decided you didn't want him. All told, it's hard to believe that any one of us could refer to such a potentially brutal interaction as a game, nor that sane and self-sufficient adults would enter into it. But we do. And we must, because at the other end of reentry is connection, and that's worth a lot of shake, rattle, and roll.

Actually, truth told, you will probably have to engage in bits and pieces of this process more than once, perhaps with many strangers, in order to develop one serious, solid, and cherished bond with a person who will undoubtedly turn out to be flawed, because in the end we all are. And then you will have the struggle to compromise and love him anyway. But by this time you will be long past the awkward uncertainty of getting naked again and into the serious relationship for which there are many other books written—some of which I've written myself.

Right now, though, you are at the precarious and interesting beginning. Between the relationship you've left behind and the new person with whom you will connect, there is an internal process and an interpersonal one. You can get better at both.

The internal process of getting naked again involves a personal evolution. Understanding and furthering that evolution—its dynamics, conflicts, and their successful resolution—is the subject of part I of this book. It is also its deeper purpose. Certainly we date again because it's a drag to sit home on Saturday night; because it's nice to have a man to dance with at weddings, to open jars, or to intervene with the car mechanic; or because they sometimes pay and that's a plus (though the cost of hair and makeup and shoes usually evens out this benefit). But expedience is not the only reason we return again and again to courtship, decked in hope and dread and fresh Botox.

Romantic life is really nothing more than a playing field; increasing your capacity to give and receive love is the prize. A sexual reawakening, some very good laughs, and the sheer pleasure of telling your girlfriends the tale are the side benefits. And happiness—packaged as quiet contentment, studded with emotional sizzle, and grounded in a sense of connection—is the point. To enjoy these fresh emotional heights, though, you will need more than a suitable partner. You need an evolving sense of yourself.

Most of us who get naked again start by shedding or losing a partner. We go from attached to alone, but that change of outward status takes awhile to percolate through to the soul. Naked can feel very chilly, and some of us rush to shelter in a quick new relationship, create a career onslaught, or take temporary, even necessary cover in the lives of our children. (A daughter's divorce can, for example, distract you from the pain of your own.) But wherever you hurry to hide out, the change of identity will creep up. It's best to be ready for it.

Even if you just stand bravely stripped and single in the world, it will still take some time to integrate the idea that this is *you*, meeting a strange man for coffee; *you*, handing cuff links to a man not your husband as you two dress after sex for a theater curtain; *you*, slow dancing at a resort party with a man who miraculously appears to have an erection. All the while the woman who lives in your mind's eye is still married, a mother, a wife, a granny. Who are you now? Who will you become? Or more likely, if it's fear whispering the questions instead of excitement—what's to become of you?

Victorian as the thought is, it does capture the sometimes overwhelming sense of uncertainty that accompanies the transition from some safe harbor to the unsheltered world of single life. Over time, if you pay attention and press through the obstacles to change, this becomes *you*, free to decide whether to spend the money on the new roof or the trip to Africa; *you*, removing the dead mouse from the kitchen floor because there's no one else there to do it and you know what, it's doable; *you*, deciding to stay, move, buy, rent, with only your adult children to natter at you about your decision; *you*, slipping your business card into some guy's pocket because at this point, why the hell not?

Getting Naked Again is about evolving into an adult single woman after you've defined yourself as part of a whole. It's about partnering again, if that's what you hope for, and about taking your clothes off in front of someone again, even if that's what you fear. It's about revealing yourself—your heart, your soul, your quirks and calcified habits, your physical droops, maternal missteps, crammed closets, and/or empty retirement funds—to fresh judging eyes. It's about acting in your own self-interest, especially when your heart is steering you off the cliff of love, or when your fear has you dug deep behind a barricade of reasons.

It's about doing all of this with a smile on your face and a strong and clear sense of yourself, recognizing:

- How the injuries and frustrations of your previous relationship shape your next one.
- Which mistaken fantasies and beliefs you may be nurturing.
- The signs that you are ready to reconnect.
- Which of the two great reentry fears drives you.
- Your most productive mind-set for dating.

In the end, like it or not, dating, commitment, and love are less about whom you meet and more about who you are. Part I of *Getting Naked Again* focuses on understanding who you are and catching up with the woman you've become.

None of that introspection is easy, especially because you'll be seriously distracted. Though it may be rough, getting naked again is also an emotional rush. After all, you are not only going back to the game of romance; you are also returning mentally to the last time you played it. Circumstances have thrown you back on your own, to an earlier solitary time in your life. You are suddenly without cover, open to the cruelty of the seven-second judgment, the evaporating e-mail friend. You are back to thinking about what to wear with an eye to how it unzips. Back to contemplating eyelash batting, phone-call waiting, and hope followed by crash followed by delicious, exuberant hope again.

In other words, you might be feeling the same wild mood swings and jailbreak giddiness you felt when you first left home. If you are coming back to life after a freezing grief, or a decade of grim marital endurance, you might just zip up a bustier, strap on your four-inch heels, and wallow in being young again for as long as you can.

But even if dating rituals make you feel temporarily twenty—with all its sexual thrill and shaky self-worth—it's still smart to use your grown-up head to steer by. True, everyone goes back into the game in his or her own way, but there are common success and failure patterns from which you can learn. There are basic dating and relationship skills in which we could all use a refresher. More important, there are mistakes you can avoid, pitfalls to steer around if only you could see them coming. And, just as every satellite needs to align itself properly to assure a successful reentry, you will need to adjust your attitude to best survive the atmosphere of romance. Part II of *Getting Naked Again*, Interpersonal Expertise, reviews each of the central questions:

- What's the best meet-and-mate advice offered by people who have been out there and succeeded?
- Who picks, who pays, who calls, who seduces in adult courtship these days?
- How do you manage your girlfriends, their husbands, the social world, and altered family expectations when you turn single?
- What are the four classic transitional relationships and what emotional needs do they satisfy?
- How can you recognize, and correct, your own emotional regressions?

This might all sound like much ado about something that depends primarily on luck and the right social connections. In fact, most of us, whether we are dating at twenty-seven or seventy, tend to obsess about the question "Where do I go to meet someone?" and ignore the rest. After all, meeting someone is the necessary if not sufficient condition to a romance, and if you believe that no one is out there, then what good is knowing the best way to proceed? Too, "Where do I meet someone?" resonates with the cherished romantic belief that meeting the right person is everything, that when it's right it's right, that love solves problems.

Meeting is a critical part of the process. Whom you are willing to meet, how open you are to meeting, to connecting, to risking the rejection that so often follows meeting, how willing you are to do the picking, how much you rely on being the one picked—all of these are crucial relationship variables for you to examine and reevaluate.

You can't ignore the meet-who-where question. But frankly,

if you focus exclusively on it—that is, if you don't look beyond the reasonable advice to

—join clubs, ask friends for introductions, pursue your hobbies, be friendly, go where the boys are, but only if you're
sure you wanna be there, to take up golf or tennis or Internet matches, to try Elderhostel travel or SilverSeniors
or Gorgeous Grandmas or some other equally chirpily
named group

you are apt to put out a great deal of effort with very little return.

After all that work, with little love to share, you will naturally come to believe that there is no one out there, all the good ones are taken, no one you want will ever want you. In other words, without thinking more deeply about what you are doing, you could easily end up with all the self-limiting convictions that make so many of us retire to our sweat suits and curl up with our cats. Getting naked again, you've determined, was a bust.

Meeting someone is a numbers game, as you've been told. But it is also more than a numbers game. It is bringing the right mind, body, and spirit to that numbers game. You are, after all, reentering after a long relationship followed by a brutal divorce (and they are pretty much all brutal, just each in its exquisitely individual way). Or you are gathering your strength to reengage after the death of a longtime partner—whether it was a partner you adored or one you tolerated and, if it was a long marriage, you surely felt some of each.

These losses might have been recent, in the last weeks or years. Or they might have been long ago, and you ignored the possibility of romance in favor of your career, your parenting responsibilities, your destructive addictions or elevating preoccupations. Whatever your individual pattern, when you reenter the game after age forty or so, you are different this time around. Your mind, your body, your emotional attitude will probably need a little conscious work, some weeding, some turning of the mental soil, before anything new can really take root.

It's not all about whom you meet. Getting naked again is, first, foremost, and maybe in the end most important, all about who you are when you meet him. And that depends, at least in part, on what sent you back out there.

CHAPTER TWO

You Bleed or You Thaw

She is wearing Prada heels with half ankle straps that keep sliding ahead of her toes. It takes all her concentration to make it to the table for this date, her first date in, oh, twenty-five years. He is wearing a matching tie and pocket scarf. The only other man she knows who wears a pocket scarf is her dad. The man she is divorcing wears flannel. This could be a good thing.

He orders wine with lunch and drops the name of several boards on which he sits. She appears properly impressed and tries to imagine kissing him. They find common conversational ground in their workouts.

He asks: "How many men at that gym hit on you?"

She fumbles: "Gee, I really don't know. I mean, I was married all that time."

He asks: "Wait. How many men have you screwed in the last twenty years?"

She admits: "Uh, one? I was married."

He: "No wonder your friend said you were looking to get laid."

Her friend? Was that the friend who asked if it was okay to give her number to a pleasant, pocket-scarf-wearing, board-sitting, wine-ordering divorced man looking to meet someone?

She's not ready for this.

A return to dating is emotional whiplash, pure and unavoidable. One hour, one month, you are entirely absorbed in the heartbreak of loss—sleeping in a partner's sweater because it still smells of him, leaving his voice on the answering machine because it comforts you to pretend he is there. And then profound and genuine feeling is abruptly interrupted by some absurd dating dilemma: When, you find yourself wondering, exactly when will you wear the great negligee you bought for your first weekend away with a new lover?

I mean, do you don it the moment you check in and sort of swan around the room for a while? Or wait until just before going to bed, when, being a man, he will be on to the sex and want the nightgown off as soon as possible? (This will pretty much be a waste because great negligees can cost as much as a large appliance and should therefore be appreciated.) Possibly you put it on after sex, but isn't he sleeping then and aren't you? Surely you could decide to do without the nightgown problem completely, but that leaves you with the naked problem. And so on.

The process of emotional recovery—from sadness to preoccupying silliness, and back again—is a normal if disorienting aspect of resuming romantic life. Certainly you are back to romantic thrill and the girlish uncertainty of your youth, back to trying to figure out what he really means when he says he'll call, back to wondering if you should say you're not free, even though you are free, just so he won't know exactly how free you are.

But then again, you're not back there at all.

You are not really back to dating again, not returned to the you of twenty-two or thirty. You are dating again, but after a serious romantic injury. The shape of your scar and the degree of your healing will influence every subsequent connection you form.

Here's what might have happened:

You were safe in the harbor of a romantic partnership and—suddenly, harsh and impossible to believe, or slowly and torturously—you lost it. Whether through the tragedy of death, the humiliation of sexual betrayal, or the dry ice of emotional dismissal, your partner left you and took with him the cocoon in which you two sheltered. You're back out here because he forced you to be.

The opposite might be true for you. Somehow, somewhere, you found the strength to leave that shelter of your own volition, recognizing that while it was safe—safe in the sense that its miseries were familiar and therefore tolerable—it was not happy, not satisfying, not alive, and therefore, in your opinion, not right. Even if you've left a harsh or unhappy harbor, it still sets you out on the open sea. Baby, it's cold out here.

Many of us were in the middle. You sort of stopped loving him and he sort of checked out and it was unraveling and you were ambivalent and then this happened and that happened and whatever finally caused the breakup—here you are, you're baaack.

Or maybe not. Neither breakups, nor widowhood, nor other life changes must send you back into romantic life if you are unwilling to go. There are plenty of ports in which to take refuge from flirtation, courtship, or sexual attraction.

Work and single motherhood are the traditional sanctuaries from the storm of sexual excitement and romantic defeat, but your own haven might have been something more personal, less universal. A preferred passion for travel or bird-watching, aging parents, financial catastrophe, or inner battles that range from addiction to eating disorders and back through depression or time-consuming compulsions—any of these emotional burdens or idiosyncrasies can keep you out of the game and inside a rocky harbor of your own creation.

Recently, though, something in you may have started to heal or begun to thaw.

Maybe the kids have finally left home and there you are, looking in the mirror and through the closet for the first time in ages. Could you, you wonder, get back in the game? Or the kids are still around, but you looked up recently and noticed that they were having sex themselves and how come they get to have all the fun? Is it really all over for you?

You had a birthday, your hormones shifted, you lost five crucial pounds, a new member of your investment group sparked some old feeling, your girlfriend met someone, it's spring, and suddenly . . . you're thinking, very privately, that if it were possible (it's not, you're sure, it's not), but if it were possible—only if you meet someone, you'll give it a try, you're considering or definitely committed—you're coming back.

And you are bringing your history with you.

Cause for a Comeback

You are starting over with a personal story, with feelings and beliefs about love, about men, women, and about yourself. Those internal elements will strongly color how you resume romantic life, what prize you seek, and whether you expect to succeed. In this sense, as in all other games, the playing field is not level. Your personal story is part of your handicap.

Certainly it matters whether you are widowed or divorced, whether you were dumped or in grateful flight. Still, there is certainly a core similarity among all of these experiences. First, each involves loss, and loss has its own emotional geometry, whatever its trigger. Every recovery from loss involves a transition, a period beautifully described by consultant William Bridges as a time when you let go of the way things used to be and somehow take hold of the way they have become. Sounds smooth enough, but Bridges emphasizes the chaotic gap between the past and future, "a low-pressure area, where all kinds of heavy weather is drawn into the vacuum left by the loss." Widowed or divorced, you are getting naked in a stormy climate.

Too, a woman newly single for whatever reason has to deal with the isolation and second-class status accorded single women without adequate fuck-you money. (Those with sufficient cash will be accorded the standing of men.)

And, widowed, divorced, or detached, you must still struggle with the fresh reality that, as the author Carol Shields observed, you are no longer first in anyone else's world order. Now you are deeply alone in the way that we all are, but can pretend not to be when we are snuggled in the sanctuary of the couple. In this sense, by whatever circumstances you arrive, single is single.

And then again, it's not. One big difference is in the element of choice, and in how society regards those not chosen. Whether you see yourself as victim or initiator will impact both your emotional state and the kind and amount of injury you sustain.

The following discussion is not meant to be a catalog of the miseries that relationships and their endings might inflict. For one thing, you know that pain too perfectly—the place it tended to lodge in your throat, your stomach, the small of your back; the way it came and went and came again when you thought you had run it to ground. Getting naked again begins, if it begins at all, someplace down the road from that pain, and it is influenced by the long shadow of the life-altering experience you've endured.

It must be said that not all relationship endings are occasions of mourning. Relief and even elation may play a part; celebration too, however privately it tends to be held. Life being the messy emotional stew we are so unprepared for it to be, some death and much divorce stirs the whole pot—relief, regret, despair, and possibility. You will naturally be some time sorting your way through this. At the end of this chapter there is a discussion of the signs and signals to identify your own progress toward readiness for a next relationship.

For now the point is only this: Coming back to romance after a divorce differs from the return after the death of a partner. You will probably carry different baggage, and, whether you do or not, the world will regard you differently.

A widow—no matter the emotional quality of her marriage—is telling a dignified story. She is regarded with a well-deserved compassion for gathering the strength and imagination to reconstruct a life after devastating disruption. Those who eventually have the courage to reconnect with romance deserve the respect they are accorded.

Divorced women and men, on the other hand, raise an eyebrow. Sometimes a whole curling upper lip. Someone wasn't good enough. Someone failed, quit, cheated, lost. The world looks you over and wonders privately—was it you? What is it about you? What invisible flaw or obvious known fault line cracked and left you standing there on that ice floe all alone? (Well, alone but for a crowd of lawyers, aging parents, damaged children, and left-behind pets all needing care and feeding and comfort themselves. But alone, nonetheless.)

It's easy to grow all too aware of this abrasive scrutiny and give in to the urge to defend yourself. "It wasn't me," you explain in earnest or in fury, "it was him/her/them. He cheated, he lied, she's a shrew, she shopped, he's sick, she's crazy." And are judged more harshly for the unevenness of your explanations. So you repackage your history to the socially acceptable, "It was both of us really." The social scrutiny doesn't stop, but you learn to tune it out. Progress.

Your own mean internal monologue may take longer to tune out. Divorced people report long conversations with themselves regarding their unlovability or the unlikelihood of finding a partner worth loving. One woman's husband of thirty-some years mentioned his unhappiness and moved out a week later. For several years after, she saw his rejection everywhere, everywhere. "I felt like the world was pointing at me when I walked down the street, saying, 'There goes that old woman no one wants.'"

Even a welcome divorce can carry with it the aroma of failure that lingers past the celebration of freedom. One woman reported, "My dad said to me, regarding my divorce, 'That's one strike. Three strikes and you're out.'" Not all of us face openly harsh judgment, but certainly every divorced person has to work to polish her social résumé when applying for the next relationship. Widows and widowers, on the other hand, can rest on their last impressive job title: loving wife; committed husband. It's better.

Some divorced people believe that it's simply preferable all around to have a dead rather than an ex-spouse. Pammy is outspoken enough to say so. "I do think it's better to have your husband die. If mine had died, I would have gotten everything. This way I got half, and the battle to get my fair share almost destroyed me. Also, I get to go places and see my husband everywhere with a younger woman. I feel like I can't heal because I'm constantly reconnecting with the pain."

If your own divorce was sufficiently agonizing, you might find yourself in sympathy with Pammy's acid assessment that widowhood is preferable. If so, for God's sake I hope you are grown-up enough to keep this to yourself. Not every honest thought bears repeating and mentioning to a widow: "You don't know how lucky you are. I'd be so much better off if George were dead" is a real showstopper.

In fact, judicious self-censoring is practice for getting naked again. Discreetly masking some pieces of yourself while exposing others is a necessary part of early dating and relationship building. In this too, widows and widowers have a natural advantage. Like all advantages, though, it comes at a price.

The death of a spouse tends to discourage ugly conversation

about that previous marriage, a nasty topic known to frequently leak onto and corrode otherwise promising second dates with divorcées. It's not just that we find it unseemly to speak ill of those who have passed away, it's also that death is the great eraser of all kinds of ill feeling in the first place.

Therein lies the hidden cost of widowhood when it comes to reconnecting with a new partner. It is natural to idealize a lost spouse

—because the hole he left makes us anguishingly aware of what we have lost;

—because memory clings to the happy times and wipes away petty irritations; and

—because love, so easily submerged by the daily abrasions of intimacy, floods back through us when those annoyances are removed and we are face-to-face with a severed attachment. The phantom limb screams. Reattachment seems to be all we could wish for.

So the widow has the problem of replacing an idealized partner with a new and very real one. She has a hole in her life whose size and shape are well known to her, and she is apt to automatically cast a new man into that gaping wound. If he fits well, these two might proceed from reentry to remarriage without missing a beat. But that beat goes on—into new stepchildren, different houses, strange rhythms, expectations, rituals. It can be a fast reconnection, but it is not necessarily an easy one.

Widowers, in particular, are legendary in their desire to remarry with dispatch. Tales of obituary scanning may be the stuff of suburban legend, but there is enough social truth in them to pay attention. Widowers regularly seek new wives to fill the role and the function, if not always the place in the heart. (Think Sir Paul McCartney for the most visible example of the urgency that can befall a man who has lost a beloved spouse, and the catastrophe such haste might create.)

"I just wanted my life to continue," sixty-eight-year-old Eli explained firmly. "I married straight out of college, a wonderful woman who never gave me a moment's aggravation. When I lost her, I retired, sold my house, and moved back to the city where I had great college years. I called an old girlfriend too, one I dated fifty years ago. She was divorced and we got together and for a minute, I thought we could pick right up there. She had too much baggage, though—grandchildren who always needed babysitting and chauffeuring. I could see right away that I would be spending my life sitting for someone else's grandchildren and I sure didn't want that. So I ended it.

"I'm still looking, though, for someone who will travel with me and go to concerts with me, the way my wife would have if she'd lived." He pauses in his story, which he'd related easily and forthrightly as any man on a mission. Then he added his postscript. "I know this much about myself. I'm no good alone. I can't be alone. And I don't want to learn to get good at it."

Widows of long and satisfying marriages often describe themselves as sustained by the relationship and its memory— an emotional support that, for many, survives death. For some time, though, that widow's path may be dogged by the common guilt of the survivor. It echoes in variations of gripping self-punishment: *"If he's not alive, I failed somehow."*

In *Chapter Two*, the play describing the internal conflict created by his rapid second marriage after the death of his spouse, the great Neil Simon tackled a variation on this perplexing piece of mental baggage. Death does not erase the guilty feeling of infidelity. Sometimes, irrationally, it enhances it. If you are widowed, you might be hampered by the same inner struggle.

"How do I love someone new without betraying my allegiance to my spouse? How do I hold on to my love for my spouse, which is all I have left of him, if I give that love away to another person? I want a new relationship, but I don't want one too." Guilt.

Guilt may smother the possibility of a new relationship because it can leave the survivor reviewing and regretting behavior from the past. The sudden death of a spouse leaves us especially prone to this obsessive review—the emergency room too late; the last words, impossible to recall or—perhaps worse—remembered as harsh, thoughtless, foolish, unintended. Life interrupted and so measured by a heedless last encounter. It takes thinking, processing, churning, and a mental working-over of the memory until it can be endured and then incorporated into your view of yourself and of your relationship. Until then, loss and guilt might close your heart to the possibility of reattaching somewhere fresh.

A death after long illness does not protect the surviving spouse from paralyzing guilt, although at least three widowers with whom I spoke mentioned that their freedom to date came directly from a sense of completion with their dying wives. Two described wives' bouts with cancer as some of the strongest times in the marriage. "We said everything we had to say to each other," said one; "It was our closest period," said the other. Both these men have approached dating with a zest that guilt tends to prohibit.

But some long slides toward death leave the survivors with guilt and exhaustion that does not automatically end with their caretaking responsibilities. One widow, checking her computer to see what Match.com possibility might have found her cute today, suddenly got up, switched gears (whiplash in action), and spoke about the weight that choked her even now, three years after the loss of her husband. "I'm guilty, will I always be guilty? I'm guilty because, through our whole marriage, there was nothing I wanted that he didn't try to give me. And he knew that I didn't want him to leave me. So he suffered to stay alive. I should have helped him go, but I couldn't." Guilt—an amorphous lump of rage and anguish and no place to direct its arrow but toward your own heart.

What may be guilt and anguish in the widow appears as rage and pain in the divorcée. Divorce leaves a bleeding hole too, but of a different nature. You don't have the problem of an idealized partner whom you are hoping to replace. Instead you probably have the demonized partner who may be hanging around. Whether he is present physically or mentally, he is in the way of a new relationship.

Perhaps your ex is deliberately visiting the grandchildren at the same time that you want to see them. Or he is still fighting with you about paying for your business degree or ignoring the insurance he's required to carry according to the divorce agreement. He has suddenly co-opted your daughter and is turning to her for sympathy when his relationship with his girlfriend is in trouble. Worse, she listens, and her betrayal stabs at you.

Some savvy single men, recognizing that you are still caught in the brutal currents of broken child-care agreements and unreliable alimony payments, stay a safe distance from you. Any new man who does get close to you is apt to be sucked into your chaotic vortex. Three in the bed is crowded, for sure.

You may be sick when you hear your ex-husband's voice on the phone, or you may be one of those who continue to call him at the slightest broken appliance. Either way, you are forced to recognize that divorce is a slow emotional and legal process that occurs in stages. For some, it begins years before the physical separation. For most of us it proceeds at best in fits and starts—forward through the splitting of the all-important stuff, backward through the occasional, predictable, yet unexpected sexual encounter. Or two.

On through the signing of the legal divorce, and still on through the lingering fantasy of reconciliation that lives in the hearts of your kids and, truth be told, sometimes in your own. This whole time that you are mentally, emotionally, and legally divorcing, some huge part of you is married, and therefore only partly available for a new mate.

Too, it's hard not to view divorce as a personal failure, even if, privately, you regard your courage in initiating the divorce as a private triumph. You may have been shocked by how much the dissolution of your marriage has affected your adult children. Their ongoing sadness and anger as they struggle to adjust to their loss, to tolerate sexual parents, new partners, stepparents, depressed, despairing, or warring parental partners—all of it puts a damper on any divorced woman's sense of personal celebration. Even if your divorce represents strength in your own eyes, you may see failure reflected in the eyes of your kids, should you dare to look.

Certainly the social world views divorce as evidence of some failure—whether failed hope, or skill, or something worse. In the end divorce is most certainly a failure of love, and, however common such defeat is, it carries a faint stigma back out into the dating world. You have to explain yourself. To them. To yourself. You have to tell the story in a way that buffs your image, disguises your outrage and injury.

The story itself, practiced and improved upon by the many requests for retelling ("So, tell me about your divorce"), can be tweaked to present the strong, tolerant, yet loving you who has learned from experience but is above-all-not-bitter. Your risk, of course, is that the story will come to conceal your personal truth, even from yourself. And you'll need that truth to reconnect better the next time.

Those who initiate divorce have one enormous advantage over widows: Initiators can gradually build a new life while clinging to the security and stability of the old. People in unsatisfying marriages pull away from partners—sometimes deliberately and sometimes utterly unconsciously—and create whole separate friendship circles, interests, relationships, lives really. At the eventual moment when the confrontation is staged, the new apartment is rented, the joint account is closed, those who have completed part of this emotional divorce have a comfortable new haven in which to ride out the worst of the storm.

Traditionally men take shelter in a new relationship with a fresh woman who will provide the sexual, social, and emotional comfort that eases a married man's transition into divorce. Divorced women also sometimes leave with a lover in tow, but a separate life in which to take refuge does not have to include another romantic relationship. There are, as Paul Simon says, "fifty ways to leave your lover." One of the classics is to invest your heart and soul elsewhere while continuing to bring your body home at night. Then one day you leave home.

For example, Carole, at forty-six, became more and more committed to environmental issues. What began as an effort to clean up a local park evolved into a political PAC supporting green candidates. Along the way Carole developed a network of friends, new competencies, and a social world where she was a welcome presence as a single woman. When she finally divorced Martin, Carole was mentally, emotionally, and socially prepared in the way few widows could ever be. In effect, she allowed herself to practice being single before she had to live it full-time. Time on the job improves performance.

By contrast, widows and dumpees may not have developed separately sustaining lives because they are living very much as part of the *we*. When *we* abruptly disappears, there's very little *I* to fall back on.

This could be the case if your own divorce story is the ugly old tale of being replaced. What if you did not initiate the divorce, emotionally or otherwise? What if you endured the marriage or delighted in it and celebrated it; what if you honored your commitment whether through integrity, innate caution, or passionate, loving devotion; and one day . . . the phone bill with the dozens of calls to another woman's number . . . the credit card with the strange charges . . . the anonymous letter . . . the well-meaning friend . . . the private investigator . . . the guilt-stricken confession . . . all followed by the tears, the emergency marriage counseling, the shock, the frantic who, why, how, when negotiation, the attempt to bend your mind around a life decaying around you and somehow you missed the signs, failed to guard against them, and now it's gone, forever gone, and you are left there.

You stand single now, left behind with the troubled children, and the house to sort through, and the friends who are rallying around, but imperfectly, who are repudiating him, but not totally, not enough, not entirely—left, in the end, alone, considering the prospect of getting naked again. But you are reentering bleeding, and that will color every encounter until you learn to see through to yourself more clearly.

Divorce after rejection is a particularly awkward story to tell because it evokes public sympathy and private speculation from your audience. Publicly you are a victim, an attractive figure to only a subset of men drawn to the needy and injured. To the rest you are a cautionary tale—filled, they fear, with understandable rage at men. Each new man hesitates, concerned that he will be your next target. Learning how to conceal that fury will be your first task when you reenter the game. But learning how to heal from it will be your more serious emotional work—and that's a longer haul.

Certainly it matters whether you chose to be back here or were tossed into the arena on your rejected butt. It matters some whether you lost the weight that was your excuse or you just stopped worrying about it. It matters whether you changed the career that kept you on the plane half the week or you just got good enough at it to add a personal life. But it only matters a little.

In the end,

—whether you've finally gotten the courage to make a leap out of the unsatisfying relationship and into life on your own;

—or the harbor dissolved under its own weight—the business
finally failed and freed you from its serfdom, the parent
died and your caretaking duty ended;

—or the kid who doesn't need you, the husband who traded
you in, or the boyfriend who just couldn't commit booted
you out into the world;

here you are. Devastated or delighted, anticipated or an unexpected shock—you are unattached, considering the prospect of
getting naked again. And you will—when you're ready.

Ready or Not

A tide of loneliness or outrage sweeps some of us out to
singles bars the night a husband packs, with the intention of
filling the other half of the bed. And some of us creep out of
our cocoon by cautious inches. Wherever you might be on this
continuum, it's helpful to recognize the general signs of emotional availability.

Of course, your own timing might be easy to spot. One
widow, Katherine, spoke for many when she said, "For a long
time I just couldn't imagine being with another man. But I
started to want a hug. I wanted someone to hold my hand. I
hate the word *lonely*. I wasn't lonely exactly, but I was lonely for
male companionship."

Readiness, though, is a process of bits and pieces. Katherine continued, "I knew I was ready for a physical relationship
because I kissed a date and I liked it. But at the same time I
felt that if I looked over in bed and saw another man's head
on my husband's pillow—it would kill me. You know, I can

date. I can be picked up at the house. But having a man hang out in my living room or sit down to watch a game and maybe sit in my husband's chair—it's just not something I could bear yet."

Even if you haven't noticed you are ready, friends and family might send a signal that it's time. True, friends tend to be ready for you to "move on" long before you feel comfortable. They are helpfully offering to clear out a husband's closet when you still cannot bear to move a sweater. Or suggesting that you "get out there" when the farthest out you feel capable of going is the video store.

Sometimes that social push, however warmly intended, is sickening. You feel judged, pressured, and misunderstood. The fact is, readiness to get naked again takes whatever time it takes. For some of us, that will mean another year, and for others it'll mean the rest of our lives. When friends are pushing you, you will have to learn to push back. What matters is your own inner rhythm.

At the same time, many people, temporarily deaf to an internal pulse, report that it was the signal sent by friends or family that moved them into the dating world.

"I knew I was ready when my son said to me, 'Mom, you need a new life. You won't know what you want—whether it's a new husband, or a friend, or to be single—until you get out there.' Maybe I was waiting for his permission?"

A widower, unaccustomed to determining his own emotional compass, relied on the kindness of his social network. "My sister lives in Arizona, so I moved there to start a new life near family. After the move, my friends decided that it was time, so they gave me the numbers of some women to call. I was enjoying my independence, but I certainly wanted someone to share my independence with."

Sometimes the readiness signal comes from a wholly unexpected source.

Your body: "I found a lump in my breast about six months after my husband and I separated. I thought 'I have to have sex again before the mastectomy.' I went right to my golf club and started making eye contact."

Your ex: "I had moved out, but I didn't know the marriage was not going to reconcile until my wife started dating."

Or someone wholly unexpected: "I ran into a young man with whom my deceased husband and I had done business. He asked me if I was dating and I said, 'Not really.' He said, 'I've wanted you for as long as I've known you.' Honestly, I got so flummoxed I started to fan myself. I'm not going to see him. I can hardly picture myself handling an older Jewish guy, much less a young stud. But it definitely awakened the sexual side of me that I thought was dead."

Meanwhile, most of us will not be able to depend on the firm intervention of family or the flirtatious come-ons of our handsome tennis partners to get the juices flowing again. We have only our inner stars to steer by. If you know what to look for, though, that should be enough.

Readiness is a suitably vague term, but basically it means that you have traveled far enough past your initial shock, numbness, pain, or grieving to assume a lighthearted social attitude—if only for the evening. Your healing is progressing successfully enough that you can play nicely with others.

Remember, though: Healing from suffering is slow, and it does not occur in a straight line. You have good and bad days,

just as you have good and bad dates. To avoid the risk of that
emotional roller coaster, some of us buy property in Numb and
live defensively. That way neither the best nor worst social interaction has any noticeable emotional impact. There's less pain
living in Numb, but having moved there, it's easy to risk frozen
forever.

If you have moved deep behind your defensive wall, you
will only begin to be ready when you feel some returning sense
of energy and spirit. Ironically, though, dating, flirting, and
sex can be restorative behaviors that reawaken your frozen life
spark. So you may have to go through the motions of life before
you are really ready, in order to stimulate readiness so you can
really engage.

If your feelings tend to flood instead of freeze, overreaction
might become your emotional MO for some time. Early good
or bad dates can then have way too much impact, because your
defenses are thinned after serious emotional injury. A literate
e-mail arrives accompanied by an attractive photo and you are
wild with hope. A fix-up shows his boorish side and you bury
yourself in junk food or wine. Whether you're frozen or overwhelmed with feeling, it takes yet more time to undo the damage caused by the pain relievers of your choice. But eventually
and with a personal push, you notice you are ready.

Readiness, by the way, is not desperation, though it's a fine
distinction, for sure. One is playful, the other grim; one is appetite, the other starvation; one is open, the other empty. You
get the picture. Don't be too hard on yourself, though. There
are flash floods of desperate need in the strongest of souls. They
pass, and we stagger on.

Remember too, that ready is a big tent. You could be ready

to start trading e-mails, but a long way from face-to-face encounters. You could be open to backseat sex but completely unwilling to risk monogamy for one more bruising go-round. You could be ripe for a special person to slip neatly into the gaping hole left by the love you lost, or prepared only for measured companionship that never again includes sexual intimacy.

You might believe you are interested in dating right up to the moment that a man appears who is interested in you. He asks if he can call and everything in you is repelled. While you are civilly scrawling some number on a card, you are thinking, *"Don't look at me. Don't notice me. For God's sake, don't call me."* Since this reaction makes no apparent sense, you will probably attribute it to something unappealing about this particular man. But when it happens a second time, you'll start to wonder, "Am I ready, or am I nuts?" You are allowed to be both, you know, and anything else in between. Reentry carries a heavy emotional load. Naturally you will teeter. Just keep moving forward.

However your emotional sands shift, readiness means that you are feeling some willingness to reengage in romantic life. Here are telltale signs:

- You are past the acute stage of heartbreak. You are no longer curled in bed weeping; no longer zombified on meds just to get yourself through the day; no longer sleepless or stuporous. You have resumed some reasonable level of your previous functioning.
- The physical symptoms of loss have subsided—the actual heart pain, stomachache, chest flutters, headaches, or whatever symptoms might be your particular body's response to

emotional injury. Mind you, they have probably not disappeared entirely, but they have eased.

- You have moved past the despairing feeling of being utterly lost, past the impossibility of imagining a future. You might not know what that future is, but you are starting to see positive glimmers.

- You notice some restoration of your crushed sense of self-worth or guilt over the death. You have fewer self-punishing thoughts, and you challenge them more when they come.

- You are getting a grip on your self-destructive behavior—curbing your drinking, monitoring your drug use, and restoring your eating to a healthier path.

- You are beyond the need to hear every obsessive detail about your ex and his new partner. (They were at the soccer game. She's brownish blond with bad skin.) And you are over the need to pass on every fresh detail to friends, past the irresistible urge to talk about him and her over and over, just to release your own pain. Now when a friend reports a sighting, you've started to change the subject.

- You have stopped fantasizing that your partner will call to say he's made a terrible mistake. (This one is really rough if you have an ex who is on the yo-yo cycle himself and keeps returning to you and leaving again, prisoner of his own ambivalence.)

- You notice that you are past the self-blaming thoughts ("I should have been more loving," "I should have had more sex," "I should have known what he was up to . . .") *and* past blaming him ("the selfish son of a bitch who destroyed our family for his own selfish reasons . . ."). You have reached some even ground where you can see that you both played a part in the relationship's unraveling.

- You've stopped analyzing your ex's personality. You just lost interest in it.

- You are no longer savoring revenge stories from others, or creating your own revenge fantasies.

- Your kids seem ready for you to date—not necessarily comfortable, but at peace with it. This includes kids from fifteen to fifty.

- You are able to look in the mirror, look through your closet, look around at your social world, and smile at some of what you see.

- You got rid of something old that you had been hanging on to—not just the old husband, but perhaps his clothes, or you redid your kid's bedroom into something for yourself, you sold the old car or finally bought a new mattress.

- You have taken active steps to sweeten your new life—you've acquired two or three new friends, gone back to school, learned a new skill or sport, improved yourself physically, deliberately expanded yourself intellectually, challenged yourself professionally, *something*.

- You can stop talking about your ex. If the rage and pain boil over at the smallest associative link, you aren't ready to date. (Dinner Date: "Sorry I was late. Traffic was awful." She: "Hell, my ex wouldn't even call me if he was late. Just leave me there to wonder if he was dead. Too bad he isn't.")

- You feel a sense of emotional divorce, of disconnection

from your past relationship. You are no longer reactive to things that used to irritate you, no longer concerned with his response to events. For some, this emotional divorce happens years before the legal separation. For others it fails to occur even years after the legal divorce. If you are still fuming, focusing, recounting old injuries and relating new ones to an audience of family or friends, then you still have this relationship at your emotional center. It won't make a new relationship impossible, but it will certainly impact its course.

- Finally, you are ready when you've stopped reliving or regretting the past. Your thoughts are directed mostly toward planning your future and appreciating your present. If you've healed to this degree, and you have even an inkling that you might want romance, you are ready to take the risk of reengaging in the game.

When you read through this list, you probably noticed references to struggles that you've never even experienced, much less overcome. Maybe you were able to endure complete domestic unraveling and still maintain a functional facade—steaming fresh vegetables for the kids left at home, surpassing your sales figures and organizing the book drive, all while you were negotiating your divorce against his shark attorney. When you recognize the depths to which other women have been brought by grief and rage and betrayal and loss—let yourself feel relieved. Things could be far worse, and you can take some pride in your emotional strength.

On the other hand, there may have been items on this bulleted list that you have not achieved and never intend to. Perhaps you will never stop blaming your ex for the end of your marriage, because, quite simply, you stuck and he didn't and that is not a fifty–fifty proposition. Fine. So be it. You don't have to hit every mark to be ready to reengage in love or sex or the messy overlap of the two.

If you are showing very few of these signals of emotional readiness, consider the pace of your progress and decide if you are comfortable with it. You might need a little help—psychological, spiritual, or physical—to move forward. Or, conversely, scale down your social expectations and give yourself more time to heal. You need more inner processing before you are able to enjoy a compliment from a balding bachelor.

On the other hand, if you are showing many of these signals of readiness, then push yourself to take a few more social risks. It's time. You're ready. In your heart, in your mirror, you are turning single.

CHAPTER THREE

Turning Single

She is having dinner with her very new boyfriend's very old friends. They are a circle of long-married couples, accustomed to dinners over the years where they are introduced to the boyfriend's latest woman. On this pleasant evening, it's her. One wife, the extrovert, is designated to scout out this newest entry.

"Do you work?" asks the wife.

"Yes, I do."

"Every day?" she says. "Good for you."

Ah, the patronizing security of the sheltered wife. Were you as bad when you were married for all those years? Were you, as Bridget Jones described, a "smug married"? Probably.

And now you've turned single. It's quite a leap.

Married and *single* are not mere legal, social, or relationship barometers for women. They are, in fact, alternate identity states involving dialogue and wardrobe change right down to a different bra. With that optional change in cleavage display comes an underlying thread of unnerving, what-am-I-doing-the-rest-of-my-life uncertainty. Become single and you fall backward to the adolescent turmoil of who-am-I-and-do-I-really-like-NASCAR-or-did-I-watch-it-because-he-did? None of this is a source of comfort, and some part of the transition is sheer clammy fear.

You may want to avoid any transformation to single female, and will stubbornly resist returning to the romance game if such a transformation is necessary. (It is.) But without developing that identity you run the risk of remaining hunkered down in your own past. And what's the point?

You know what's behind you, what you've left, and what you've lost. Might as well grit your teeth, face forward, and figure out how you personally are going to turn single. It's what's ahead.

Turning single, though, involves a shift of perspective that might rewrite your past, recast your future, or redefine some central aspect of your sense of self. Naturally, that'll take some time to master.

Your transformation from one role to the next is not necessarily synchronized with your actual change in relationship status. That is, "feeling married" or "feeling single" may not actually coordinate with what you *are.* Getting in sync with your new single social identity, feeling comfortable with it, and, even better, seeing it through positive eyes—all of this is part of what makes getting naked again plain work.

It's possible that every piece of your life changed when your harbor crumbled. Some men and women immediately sell a home, quit a job, dissolve a company, move to another coast, a different climate, an alternate lover and lifestyle. These abrupt changes of circumstance might be forced upon you—the old house needed two paychecks, the old neighborhood was way too close to his new girlfriend, the old job required more concentration and energy than you have been able to muster in many months. You might have lost it all, right around the time that you lost love.

Other people initiate these changes of their own accord, often contrary to the advice of friends and relatives who typically caution against impulsive life decisions. Some of us quit, move, sell, re-create ourselves because observable action is the way we communicate a difference to our inner spirit. Think of it as a conversation a person is having with herself, but in code. She is the actor (or, analysts might say, the acter-outer) who becomes someone new first by doing something new, and then by absorbing the identity of what she's done. (I am sitting on a stool at a bar making friendly/flirty conversation with a man who has bought me a drink. A part of my brain is in running commentary—"Oh look, I am now a woman who sits at bars where men buy drinks and I can think of something to say. Hey! I'm becoming single. Hey! It's not so bad.")

Action with little or no reflection is a high-risk way to shape any life, but it works sometimes. If you act on impulse—marry the next lover the month after you meet him; cut off all your hair, sell the house, and join an environmental commune; quit your job, move to Florida, and become the party planner you always wanted to be—and it turns out great, you will be congratulated for your courage and decisiveness. You will then speak with conviction about the need to follow your gut.

Should that same gut instinct turn out to have been largely

composed of rage and panic, and the decisions that stemmed from it pretty much made things worse, well, you'll blame yourself or blame your divorce or your change in medication and try not to admit your regrets to your friends. The thing is, it's impossible for any of us to say in advance whether our gut is inspired by wise instinct or craven fear. It's a safe bet to assume they are both at work.

Many people, understanding the slow process of self-awareness and unwilling or at least not imaginative enough to act without it, will maintain every aspect of life that they are not forced to abandon. If you are one of those women, you will continue to wake up in the same bed, although now you wake up in it alone. That might be anguish or exquisite relief, but it is still, in fact, alone. You might continue arriving at the same office, volunteering with the same committees, working out at the same gym. Your routine is intact, but the person who is following that routine is in process. You are in the process of turning single.

I Once Was Half but Now I'm Whole

The first person—probably in the end the most important person—with whom you will have to get naked again is you. Self-exploration might have been an old interest, pursued vigorously in your twenties when worrying about your boyfriend and fighting with your mother sent you straight to therapy to figure out what was wrong with them. And, incidentally, yourself.

Over time, though, you sidelined the question of what conflicts really motivated you and whether your father was a functional alcoholic or just a son of a bitch. Those concerns were replaced with the daily, consuming, and often quite captivating treadmill of career building, marriage, and motherhood. You figured you'd get back to self-reflection right after you solved the problem of why your husband was charming to his friends but a silent grump with you. Or why he complained that you two never had sex when it seemed to you that all he wanted was sex, and what about what you wanted? Or whether he was right that your son was not ADD, just out of control, or whether you were right and your son needed professional help? Or whatever else were the preoccupying marital conflicts of those very full years.

Those overscheduled, figuring-out-dinner years of homework wars juggled around the demands of your work would have drawn to a close in any event. You used to worry about what life would be like when the kids moved out (but secretly you thought they'd never go that far) or when you stopped working (but it seemed unimaginable that you'd ever be able to afford that) or when your mate retired (AAAUGH). But whatever it was going to be—sell the house and move to Ashville; finally have sex during the day; or continue to successfully avoid each other in the manner you two have perfected over the last decade, with him watching TV in the living room and you curled protectively with a book on the bed—it was going to be *together.*

It was going to be the two of you, in love or on eggshells, but together. He would be the one who saw you without the wig if you had to have chemotherapy. You would be the one who drove him back and forth to rehab when he needed his knee replaced. Grim or glad, he would be the last person you saw at night and the first person you saw in the morning.

And now—not.

If midlife is a crisis, then turning single after widowhood or divorce is the crisis of midlife on steroids. More has diminished than the mothering content of your days. Turning single means you've lost your frame.

Good or bad—partners set certain boundaries. We train each other, over time together. These habits are acceptable, tolerable. Those—well, no, not unless you want to pay the price of a partner's disapproval. Which you did sometimes and he did sometimes, but mostly you both let them go. Over time the character of *we* takes shape. We enjoy Thai food, read these magazines, watch this particular evening news. We vacation here, shop there, and paint every living room we ever own the very same peachy beige. It's our color. We also have the same arguments over the same differences, whether political (Clinton was a liar. No! Clinton was a love.) or highly personal (Why do you always have to be right? Well, why can't you stand it when I am?).

Lose a long-term *we* and you are automatically stripped bare. You are hunting for *I* and *I* is not always immediately identifiable. For one thing, you may have felt over the years that *we* looked a lot more like him than it did like you, especially if you are one of those women who feels she loses her identity once inside a relationship. (Yes, there is some other type of woman. You may even become her.) Whether you welcomed this surrendered identity or fought it fiercely during your whole relationship, it doesn't matter much now. *We* is no more. The search for *I* is on.

Betsy was fifty when her autocratic husband attended a high school reunion and fell in love with his very rich, very skinny childhood sweetheart. Seems they discovered many old ties and created a few new ones at five-star hotels all over the East Coast. "I hate to say that I don't know what I resented more. Yes, the betrayal killed me, shocked me. You know that familiar story. But it was sickening to me too, that he escaped our life of financial struggle and I was stuck back in it. He stepped right out of our debt, our old car, our inability to take a vacation. I had to get through month after month after month of boiling anger. I had to try to hide that sick fury from my kids because I didn't want to infect them. When the anger ebbed enough, I had to find the energy to pick up whatever pieces of myself I could salvage.

"I couldn't even think of a date for at least two years. I was so busy figuring out, 'Okay, let's see. I've been ripped in half. What's left? How can I feel like a whole person again? Where am I without him?' It was as basic as, 'What do I eat? What time do I go to bed?' I swear every step was a working-through."

Betsy is telling me this story at lunch, and the thing I notice is that she is very, very skinny herself. She has always been one of those lean, elegant women who can tie scarves, but now she is flat-out skinny, much as she has described her husband's new lover. Is she competing? I wonder. Or is it that she just doesn't eat anymore, hasn't had an appetite for the last year or two? Or is it something worse?

I ask her about it, very carefully because I wouldn't want to cause this woman an iota of additional injury. But Betsy is amazingly resilient, and she only laughs. "I've just always been one of those people who melts away under stress," she says. "But I'm careful to be healthy and I think the curves will come back when sex and love are around again. I'm starting to believe that's in my future, because my youngest leaves for college in the fall and there's a little click in my brain that says that's the right timing for me.

"My husband was ready to leave when he walked out. I don't know how long he'd been getting ready, but he definitely had a head start on me. He may have moved out, but it was at least another year and a half before I could think of myself as *not married*. I was a wife. I just stayed a wife in my head, although a very unhappy, angry wife, a wife who was cataloging all the things her shit of a husband was doing now." She's laughing now, at herself. "You know what—I'd probably been keeping that same shit inventory on and off for all the twenty-seven years of our marriage, so it really didn't seem so strange to me.

"During those months of Still Married To The Man, I was the old Betsy—tiptoeing around him and trying not to get him mad and kind of waiting for permission to make a change in the house, or plan a trip with the kids, or, I don't know, whatever. I'd run things by him to see his reaction and he'd be reasonable or nuts, depending, and I would be nervous and not eating, my usual. We were divorcing, but we were doing our married dance. It's so familiar, you know, so rehearsed. I just couldn't seem to find my own rhythm. For a long time I wasn't even listening.

"When it came, and I started to return to myself, it came in inches. It's still coming, veeerrry slowly. Maybe the first thing I did, as ridiculous as this sounds, is I took a cooking class. I am a lousy, bored cook, but I always secretly wanted to channel Martha Stewart if I had time. Well, I had time. My youngest was with his dad every other weekend and that left me with blank Saturdays, so I just signed up, even though I have no one to cook for. I learned how to make shrimp scampi, so I decided to invite four friends over to eat it. They did, it wasn't bad. It was even a little fun. That's how bitty my single steps have been.

"Right after that dinner, a friend reported to me that my husband and his new girl were inviting our old friends to his birthday party and no one knew whether to go or not. I got a, a, I don't know, a rage hurricane. Did they figure they'd take every part of my life? The anger gave me some courage, so I surveyed everything he'd left at the house—and that was plenty, because he figured I was good for storage and he'd get around to moving it all when it suited his social schedule. I decided a year of being someone's storage locker was long enough, so I put it all in green garbage bags and drove it to a women's shelter. Fitting, plus I got the tax deduction. Yes!

"So, the scampi, then the cleansing, and now the house was mine. I took over the closets and that was fun. Say what you will about divorce, more closet space cannot be undervalued. It was my first glimmering vision of the possible pleasures of being single. I've gone on from there."

Betsy finished her story and ordered crème brûlée for dessert. She ate it.

The Cheese Stands Alone

You might imagine that turning single would be a whole lot easier for those women who chose separation and divorce than it is for those of us who feel we were pretty much thrown out of the plane. ("Good luck to you. Hope you can fly. Good-bbyyyyyyeeee.") And you'd be right. It is easier. But it's not entirely a slam dunk.

A woman who initiates divorce may hamper herself with the same haunting vision that forever cements other women to unhappy relationships. For too many of us, *single woman* evokes images of unsheltered, unwanted, unloved, insecure—pretty much your basic bag lady, both economically and socially. "I don't want to be single," "I don't want to start over," "I don't want to be out there," are cries from the heart of women who feel stuck—can't make their ongoing relationship better, can't move apart because envisioning life alone feels worse. Alone forever is a fear that certainly keeps many marriages intact, so some would say that's for better, not for worse. You can judge that for yourself.

The point is that turning single is a step down in the minds of many women, including some of those who choose to leave of their own accord. Even those who welcome escape from a conflict-filled marriage may cringe at their new social status. The fact is, you cannot successfully turn single if you nurse the idea that it means turning into a loser. And an awful lot of us become single with that idea. We get over it, though.

Barbara, for example, is a sixty-three-year-old artist and socialite who makes single look very good. She's been at it for fifteen years, has enjoyed and suffered over a series of boyfriends, and, to the best of my knowledge, has never missed a party, an opening, or a New Year's Eve—whether she had a lover along or not. She knows how to do single, and she was able to point out the internal obstacles women create that must be overcome.

"Last week," Barbara said, "my buddy Gordon invited me and a friend of his who had recently been widowed to dinner. He invited two other couples that she hadn't met, because he thought she'd enjoy the company. She called Gordon the night before the dinner to make sure that he let his other guests know that she was a widow.

Otherwise, she felt they would think it strange that she was there without a man.

"Her call reminded me of the whole internal monologue I carried on when I first divorced. I couldn't eat in a restaurant—it would look weird eating alone. I wouldn't go to a movie; in fact I barely left the house on Saturday night because I went back to being mentally seventeen and thinking of it as date night. I thought I was pathetic, so I figured everyone would think I was pathetic and I spent a lot of time hiding out.

"Finally, I learned two things. One: Nobody knows who you have in your life. Nobody knows what you are thinking and where you are going after you leave the party. And as long as you have a smile on your face, nobody really cares. Two: Yes, some people may see you as the dumpee you woke up feeling like this morning. But others will see you as sexy, strong, interesting, and enviably free to come and go as you damn well please. In other words, they'll see you in the same flattering light that shines on single men. But of course, you have to sell that image to yourself first."

The best part of talking to Barbara is that she doesn't bother to make a speech about how you shouldn't care what other people think. Of course you shouldn't. But on a bad day, you do. She's got a plan for dealing with it. Go forward.

You cannot envision the tremendous upside of single if you maintain the idea that single is something you "go back" to. You might start out with that thought, as perhaps we all do. But, as Barbara pointed out, thinking of herself as going back was the biggest mistake she made. "In the beginning, I couldn't get a fix on what to do with my life because I felt like the clock had turned back and I was trying for a do-over. Re-meet. Re-mate.

Re-create. I was even thinking then, maybe Procreate. I was defi-nitely a little bit nuts. But none of it was working. I was spend-ing a lot of time killing time.

"Eventually I had to grapple with that deadly Oprah-ish question—'What do I want?' That was easy to answer at twenty-five. I wanted what we all wanted, what I was supposed to want, what biology and my mother mapped out for me. At forty-eight, it was much tougher to answer. Seemed only natural to go back to when I felt sure and assume it all still applied. But it didn't."

Your transformation from married to single gains momen-tum when you take on the difficult task of figuring out how you have evolved. Even if you've been static for many years, even if it feels like emotionally you have just been sitting still or, more likely, concentrating on other things—you have been develop-ing, changing. It takes insight, time, and self-testing to be able to answer the question, "Who did I become while I was standing here ironing?"

Some of us answer the question through dialogue with a therapist, some through yoga, and some through prayer. Some women test twenty hobbies, hikes, classes, and galleries and en-dure many private what-am-I-doing-here tears in the car on the way home, searching for answers to the simple questions "What do I care about?" "What do I actually enjoy?" and, probably the most central, "Where can I meet people I'd want to do it with?"

Other women turning single reinvent a life built around the same central passions that sustained them as a couple. If you and your mate loved travel or art collecting, home remodeling, so-cial activism, or long bike trips, you might continue to immerse yourself in these occupations as a single woman. They are at the heart of your identity, and they will be at the hub of the life you are creating. But doing them without that partner will make the doing very different—perhaps too painful to endure, perhaps exhilarating. Probably, at the very least, the familiar pastimes will be comfortable for a while, and that has a lot to recommend it at this emotional stage. Self-discovery needs a comfort zone to rest up in.

The questions from which self-discoveries emerge are huge ("What is God's plan for me?") and quite prosaic ("If the bedroom is all mine to decorate, do I still like French Country?"). They might be spiritual ("How should I use the time that's left to me so that I will feel my life mattered?") and perhaps less elevated ("Do I want bigger boobs?"). That each of these questions can occur to the same woman, and that it is not unheard of for them to cross her mind on the same day, is just one measure of the complexities of turning single. And frankly, for some it's the fun of it.

For most women, though, turning single occurs when we are emotionally raw, and so it is nothing close to fun. Changing any aspect of the old life can be loss upon loss, as it is for the widow or widower who is comforted by the books left on the nightstand the day a beloved partner was moved to the hospital for the last time. Think of Joan Didion, explaining in her chronicle of grief, *The Year of Magical Thinking*, her inability to give away her deceased husband's shoes, because her husband would need shoes when he came back.

For others, outward change might represent a frantic repudiation of every shared aspect of *we*. "On the day we were done, finally done, I threw away the sheets, the glasses, pretty much everything he picked out. I even changed my toothpaste brand.

Then I went out," one woman told me, explaining how she did not transition into turning single, she simply "woke up free."

Most of us eventually take some concrete steps to mark out our new territory. You might take that step consciously and deliberately, as did one wife of forty-one years, who divorced and returned to her maiden name. "I went back to my maiden name even though it was different from my children. I felt that in my marriage, my husband was controlling and made decisions for our family completely autonomously. I hated that. My maiden name gave me more of a sense of my own self, finally." No cheese standing alone here—this woman turned single and took steps to announce herself. That'll work.

Physical change works too. Are women hardwired to face life's blows with more spirit on a good hair day? Or are we socialized into overemphasizing our looks at the expense of, say, world peace? If you are turning single, who cares, because the fact is you will do it better if you feel like you look better—and *feel like* is the operative term.

One ugly little truth we prefer to ignore is that the single version of you might have looked a tad more attractive than the married person you morphed into. Many women who turn single morph back. It's a bonus and creates a moment when life might start to be fun after all.

Ayline reflected on her process of emerging from mourning. "I was so lost when my husband died that I didn't want to leave the apartment. It was a year of gray. I just couldn't face being without him, and a part of it was I couldn't face being single. I know I'll never have what I had with Jack, but I didn't want to be alone in that apartment forever. I thought if I looked different it would give me confidence—and it did.

"I used to look *married*—you know, not bad, just married, with short salt-and-pepper hair and letting myself be a little bit rounder than I needed to be. When I started to face my life without him, I let my hair grow, turned blond, got to the gym, and you wanna know what? I felt a lot better. I don't know if I actually look better, but I sure feel like I do."

Some women just make a change in style.

"I stopped wearing those old formless clothes made out of that nasty flax material."

"I traded my Mephisto walking shoes for a pair of Manolos. I still can't figure out what I want my future to be like, but I've decided I want to spend it in high heels, having sex."

Others who can afford it (and plenty who can't) make a substantial change via plastic surgery.

"What did you do to ease your transition to being single?" a California entertainment attorney was asked.

"I went immediately to a plastic surgeon."

"What did you have done?"

"Everything. Damn, I look good."

"Damn, I look good" is the state of mind for which you are aiming, if you are turning single and considering a return to the game of courtship. That attitude may or may not result from your personal adventures in plastic surgery. It might result from your suddenly surprisingly easy divorce diet, thanks to which the fifteen pounds you've always struggled with disappear along with your husband (who really was a fathead, come to think of it), or it might accompany many months of grinding work on the treadmill. Whatever outer changes you make that restore a certain sexy swing to your walk, some inner slapping around will be necessary too.

"I know I'm not as tight as I was when I was thirty," Ayline continued to explain to me. "I have a C-section scar, a gallbladder scar, cellulite, an elephant stomach, the list goes on. But I had to face up to it and decide that this was the best my body could be now, and it would be good enough, and you know what? It is. I test-drove it with a couple of men and was reminded that their standards are waaaay lower than mine. My body really is okay with them. Damn. I must look good."

So turning single is about how clearly you see and about how good you feel you look. Too, it might occur with an open heart or a completely closed mind. Joan, for example, ignored single until it caught up with her. "I felt single only very gradually. My elixir is work, so as soon as I decided to get a divorce I pumped up my work and just started to do more. My plate was so full, I was so overextended, there wasn't time to feel anything, much less single. Besides, I always had a full life of my own, always went places by myself, so it didn't feel like that much of a change for me in the beginning. You know, walking into a room alone is always a little bit challenging, but only for the first minute and a half until you see someone you know. I was already pretty good at that.

"But then it kind of caught up with me. I wasn't lonely, but I was suddenly *alone*. I do have lots of people in my life, but without a partner I don't really have another head there who shares the problem and can help with whatever it is. It's not that I can't figure out what to do about a problem. I can. I'm good at that. But I just like the feeling of saying to someone, 'Now what are we gonna do?' Without that, I felt . . . single."

Joan was able to throw herself into her professional identity, but women without that professional shelter may have a different struggle. Kim related, "I came to being single kicking and screaming. I did not move. I did not get surgery. But I did work very hard to figure out who Kim was. I had a lot of therapy because I wanted to identify myself as something more than my kids' mother. I bet if they had been younger, I would have just fallen into that. Luckily they didn't need me to center around them, so that helped me focus wider.

"I have been a traditional stay-at-home mom and it's what I most wanted to be. If my husband came home at nine, I waited to have my dinner at nine. When he left me, I didn't know what else to do, so I just kept doing what I always did—turning up at the kids' basketball games and making the holiday dinners and inviting all the same people I always had. I held my head high and went everywhere by myself, but it was to all the same places. My friends stood by me and life continued. I can whine and feel sorry for myself with the best of them, but I keep it a secret.

"My biggest breakthrough came the first Saturday night that I allowed myself to rent movies and stay home. Every Saturday night of my married life we went out—it was part of my myth of what you do when you are married. When my husband left, I put a huge effort into going somewhere with my friends on Saturday night because I wanted my life to just keep on, no matter what. One night, when no one was available, I allowed myself to stay home, and it was fine. That's when I started to think this new life could be comfortable."

Your answer to the question "What do I want my life to be now?" will evolve as your identity develops, a Polaroid that reveals itself in its own time. In the end you will turn single the way we all do—in inches and giant leaps, two parts shortening your skirts, three parts sorting through the overwhelming paperwork and problem solving of a life suddenly unpartnered. Add to those outer fumbles some ill-defined but crucial internal part where the path ahead is completely clouded and you dodge, debate, and hack your way through to the light.

You can add romance to this melange—if you can figure out a productive way to get your head into it.

CHAPTER FOUR

Getting Your Head in the Game

I just can't get the scenario. What am I dating for these days? I don't need a man to come sit on my couch or play with my remote. I certainly don't need someone to introduce to my children. My mind goes instantly to the thought of someone moving in or marrying me, but I think that's only my years of Italian good-girl training. When I really analyze it, there are two things I need a man for and that's what I'm dating for—dinner and sex.

— Donna, forty-eight, gratefully divorced for
three years, living with three teenage sons

Unfortunately, the minute I separated I wanted to go out and find a new husband. A lot of it is just about being held and supported, but I guess some of it is about money. And that's annoying. It doesn't even make logical sense, because I have enough money to live, and my kids are taken care of too. But there's something about that cushion of absolute financial security you can get from being with a man that I just can't imagine being without.

> — Jessie, fifty-three, divorced for five years and
> engaged for one

There's not much in my life I would alter for the sake of a man. I do date from time to time, but I'm just looking for the ways that a man might add to my life, not for the things he'd force me to give up. So far, there aren't many ways.

> — Georgette, sixty-one, widowed for two years
> after thirty-two years of marriage

If I ever sleep with a man because he has money, I don't want to wake up and know myself in the morning. But I know what I want, what I still want, what I will always want. I have my dream of love. And I want to find it before I run out of time.

> — Norma, fifty-eight, whose live-in lover of
> fifteen years left abruptly last Christmas

*A*nd you? If you are getting your head back into the game, certainly you should be clear on your preferred prize, right?

Right in theory. Honorably intentioned friends, a troop of helpful psychologists, and every New Age guru east of the Law of Attraction will advise you to be perfectly focused on what you want, if only to maximize your chances of getting it. You might even reasonably expect—being older, more experienced, and presumably more self-aware—that you will be able to take this advice. Well, forget it.

That advice will work for your daughter, but it does not apply at this moment to you. And this is not your daughter's dating guide.

For one thing, your daughter is or was under the gun of the biological clock. She is seeking (if only in the back of her mind and the front of yours) a decent partner with whom to build a life, a man with whom to share the burdens and enjoy the blessings. Your daughter is certainly most apt to find that man if she keeps her goals clearly in mind and so avoids the time-wasting pitfalls of sexy bad boys, permanent commitment-phobes, charming alcoholics, and all those other emotional cul-de-sacs that sidetrack so many single women. You did your best to remind her to keep her eye on the prize, and now you might have darling grandchildren to show for it. Or not.

The point is, you knew at least the outlines of the prize for your daughter, just as you had an idea of your own goals at twenty-five or thirty-five when you were last dating. But you yourself are now in a whole new movie. Who knows what role a man, or men, might play?

For example, a married boss can offer a twenty-seven-year-old woman a long romantic affair, a great deal of suffering, and the chance to look up at forty and contemplate single adoption. Turning down that offer should be a no-brainer. (It's not, but it sure should be.) Meet that married man when you are sixty-three and his offer of fabulous, all-expenses-paid travel and an emotional confidant is something to consider. Sure, it will still lead to heartbreak, but now you know you'll survive it and a great trip is nothing to sneer at. So you might choose to keep it in mind.

On the other hand, you might have been the victim of just such a married man, only unfortunately you were the one married to him. So you'll have something quite different to say when he tenders his invitation. Either way, though, your perspective is entirely different from your view at age thirty.

This change of focus, this open agenda, this exploration of what is being offered, rather than an insistence on what you need to get—it's all contrary to how you have dated and/or loved in the past. This is probably the first time in your life that you have been free to date without a plan, to learn what feels good to you. You have a shot at identifying what will work for you, if you can relax into being open enough to learn. And that takes more time than most of us allow.

Oh, you may know for certain five things you don't want—each of which reflects a mistake you made with your ex that you have vowed not to repeat. Or you might know what you long for—anything from recapturing the sense of comfort and devotion you shared with a husband who tragically died last year to simply sex again before you die, and this time on top.

You might have developed a clear wish list (a stepfather for the kids; a man who doesn't watch football; husband material, lover potential, cultural companion, or simple sidekick) or harbor only the vaguest notion. But the fact is, at this stage it doesn't matter what you think about what you want. Because it's probably too soon to know.

This difficult idea—that our own needs and desires, like the darker dynamics of a relationship, can only become clear over time—is a frustration for so many of us. We try hard to rush the process, making pros-and-cons lists of traits for potential mates, creating arbitrary screening devices for online sifting (no one under forty or over six foot three, no one who believes that his seven-year-old could paint a Jackson Pollock). We overanalyze prospects, seeking to read the tea leaves of relationship problems. ("He summers in the mountains and I couldn't imagine giving up the beach. Next.")

We ask intimate, anxious questions on third dates—*"Do you see yourself marrying again?" "Do you mind living with older children?" "Do you own or rent?"*—in awkward nods toward romantic efficiency. The questions are important, eventually. But the answers, early on, are pretty much useless, and the mere asking casts the inquisitor in an unattractive light.

You feel the need (and you've been advised) to project years ahead, in an effort to select a partner who will end up where you think you might be going. But you are at a crossroads, and you might well end up someplace else entirely. And so might the pleasant, guarded man with whom you had coffee this morning, the one on whom you decided not to waste your time.

You, and he, and all the rest of us who have been deliberately or unexpectedly cut loose from our moorings, are *in process*. You are just resuming romantic life. *Just* might be a period of months or years since your last relationship ended, or it could be hours. Whatever your pace, one thing is still true. You are just beginning to get naked again. What you want, what you need, and certainly what you prize will only become evident over time and with experience.

You may begin by husband hunting and be surprised to find yourself in a passionate fling with your totally inappropriate Cuban tour guide. (That was some tour.) You firmly believe that no man over fifty is appealing, then find yourself having sexual fantasies about the seventy-five-year-old surgeon who sits on your condo committee. You meet a man online who shares your science-fiction fascination and for once you don't try either to make him into your boyfriend or cross him off the list. You just talk science fiction and your life is better for it.

In other words, reentering the dating world is a moment of opportunity. If you use that moment to focus narrowly on some relationship goal, you will measure each potential connection against that end and, of necessity, say no a lot. No—this guy is too self-centered, too dull, too screwed up to waste time with. Try again.

Your initial judgment might be correct, but the net effect of all those nos will be to exhaust your energy and snuff your hopes. And your occasional yes might tilt you emotionally toward nuts and desperate. The whole roller-coaster hell of the process could send you back to the bleachers, wounded again and maybe worse. No, the romantic attitude of "focus on your goal" does not stand the test of practice at this moment in your life.

You need to change your mind. Start by inching yourself free of three insidious fantasies.

Three Fantasies

Once upon a time a devoted wife and mother was dumped by her callous, self-absorbed husband whose nasty streak she had endured for twenty-three years—for the sake of her children. When he left her for a pole-dancer-turned-nutritionist, our heroine was bereft. Eventually she was broke as well, due to a mediocre divorce lawyer and her own fear of the fight. Her kids were sympathetic to her plight, but Dad had the money and the ski house, so they tended to brunch with her and vacation with him.

Sealed away in a one-bedroom condo tower that was all she could afford, our heroine was sad, isolated, and resigned to her fate. Then one day she went into a shoe store, where the owner invited her for a cup of coffee. Turned out he owned a chain of shoe stores. Turned out he fell madly in love with her and married her and took her off to a brand-new castle that he was hoping she would redecorate. He had a big budget but no nasty streak. And they lived happily ever after, with a beach house that had enough room for her kids and the grandchildren. Plus, the pole dancer dumped the ex. The end.

There is someone for whom this actually happened. Okay, it wasn't a shoe store. They met over a bridge game. But the point is that on some rare occasions, with no effort at all, a deserving middle-aged woman is rescued by a prince. It happens, just as some people win the lottery. But neither occurs often enough to plan a life around. And that's what too many women (and a fair number of men) attempt to do.

There are three great dreams that swim just below the surface of our renewed forays into love. These hungry fantasies are the Loch Ness monsters of our single psyches—glimpsed, rumored, suspected, but never really surfacing long enough for capture and examination. We do need to capture them, though, and hold them up to the clear light of rational review. Otherwise these deep wishes create powerful emotional currents, shaping unrealistic expectations, forcing us to poorly examined decisions, creating unnecessary disappointment and its accompanying pain. You've already had plenty of pain. Let's eliminate some.

Three widespread fantasies are:

- That my family and friends will provide.
- That my children only want me to be happy.
- That the right man will heal my hurt and fix my life. (And the right man might still be my ex . . .)

These three wishes share a common theme, namely the longing for protection and support. There's nothing pathological about such a longing. It's only natural to wish for loving shelter when you find yourself emotionally at sea. It's when that longing becomes expectation that we get into difficulty.

In chapter 6 we will talk in detail about the changes in friendship that occur when you turn single. There's a continuum of support offered by family and friends to a member of their circle who is suddenly solo, just as there is a wide range of need that a newly single woman may or may not be willing to expose. Whether your circle overwhelms you with care or abandons you with cruel indifference, one hard thing is almost always true: They cannot do dating and romance for you. And a part of you wishes they would.

You wish they'd come up with someone to date, or at least include at brunch someone to flirt with. You wish they'd remember you on Saturday night, or at least on a holiday—or just call for a movie from time to time because it's quiet at your house these days and nights. You wish they'd find a way to keep you included in the social world of couples, that social world that so often closes its doors to single women.

You hope that friends and family would make these efforts and frankly, quite often, they do. But it's not enough, it can't be enough, and that's where your fantasies get in the way. In the end we reenter the world of single adults on our own, with, at best, a nudge from those who love us and some cheering from the sidelines. They can watch and help, but they can't make it happen. For that, you're on your own. Bite that bullet, and you will waste a lot less time waiting for someone else to do something about your life.

When, bit by bit, you do something about your romantic life, you hope and imagine that your children will celebrate. There's no one for whom you've done more, so it's only natural for you to fantasize that now your happiness will be your children's priority. A perfectly understandable fantasy—but prepare for a far more complex reality.

Nora Ephron nailed it when she observed, "If I gave my children the choice between me, blissfully happy in Hawaii or suicidal in the next room, they would go for the next room every time." And so, I'll bet, would yours.

Ephron was reacting to the truth that children tend to want their mothers to be mothers first, and to be women with social needs, interesting dates, great trips, or satisfying sex lives a far distant second. Ironically, the more selfless and doting your style of mothering has been to this point, the harder it may be for your children to allow you to put your own needs first.

One divorced mom, proud of her weight loss and new wardrobe, was brought flatly down to earth by her daughter, a college senior who broke down sobbing one night over spring break. "I come home and find you looking anorexic in mini skirts," she sobbed. *"I want my mother back."* Don't be too surprised if your forty-year-old son sends the very same signal. Some of us are never too old to want our mothers back.

Of course the individual variation is huge. All the pre-divorce, pre-widowhood family dynamics will come into play—the communication patterns, family secrets, long-standing battle grounds, sibling rivalries, and loving traditions that make up your family will impact the way in which each child responds to your efforts to make a new life. So will the intimacy and strength of your relationship as well as the autonomy and generosity of each individual child.

Too, your child's developmental level has something to do with his ability to be happy on your behalf rather than needy on his own. In theory, a child who is launched into her own life and her own marriage should be more readily able to support your evolution than a child who is still living at home interviewing every date as a potential stepfather. But that is only theory, and many a married sister has called her brother complaining about Mom's new boyfriend, or the hemlines on Mom's new skirt.

It's also true that children root for your happiness according to how each child is mourning the parent who left. Date a widower and you will quickly sense how ready or not his children are to see their mother replaced. Some children of widows or widowers push a potential relationship right out of the family circle, offering overt disapproval or the subtle signs of rejection. Your own children will have their own timetable for healing, and, while they want you to be happy, their own emotional needs are pressing.

In the case of divorce, all timing bets are off, because your child's sincere desire for your happiness bumps up against the nearly universal fantasy of reconciliation harbored by children of divorce. It doesn't matter how irrational or how unconscious, it doesn't matter how adult your child—the fantasy of Mommy and Daddy somehow loving each other and reuniting the family is a stubborn pebble that slightly irritates the soul of even the most generous and loving of children.

And let's not forget that if an inheritance is at stake, any new relationship might threaten an adult child's sense of financial well-being. Money is tougher to talk about in our society than sex, so your child's feeling of financial vulnerability might cloud his joy at any prospective new union, and it might be that neither of you can address the problem objectively.

Bottom line? Yes, your child will support your happiness. But that wholehearted support may well be tempered by one of three fantasies of her own:

- I want my mom to stay my mom.
- I want the money to stay my money.
- I want my parents to reconcile.

Recognize these fantasies and you can deal with them sensitively and directly. If you ignore these possible conflicts or, more likely, resent them, you are apt to make relationships with your kids worse at a time when you need them to be better. It's the fantasy of their supportive joy that gets in your way. Recognizing that what's good for you might be threatening to them helps you act to soothe the threat.

Finally we have to confront the romantic fantasy that can be most damaging: the dream of being rescued by a loving man who will provide emotional and financial support and protection. That man is the prince of the Cinderella story; he is a new version of that idealized spouse of whom death cruelly deprived you; he is a resurrection of the man who loved you once but somehow vanished over the course of your marriage; he is a fulfillment of the adoring father you longed for in place of the critical one you got, or the lover you hoped would dote in the way that your adoring dad has. He is the man we've mentally profiled who sometimes keeps us from loving the actual man who comes along, one who cannot measure up to our romantic longings.

You have probably wrestled this fantasy to the ground once or twice already in your lifetime—when you went through early dating and disappointment, or in the first years of marital struggle when your perfectly good mate turned out to be so different from what you expected or felt you deserved.

Many men, by the way, have a masculine version of this fantasy. She's the millennial version of the Stepford wife—a woman more accomplished than the original, perhaps, but still at heart so gratified by serving and pleasing her man that she has no annoying demands of her own.

You probably came up against these conflicting fantasies when you were negotiating your last relationship. Men wanting to be nurtured by an uncritical, doting wife marry women who want to be supported by strong, adoring husbands. Then we disappoint each other and work out a relationship. The first thing that has to go, in order for that relationship to work, is the romantic fantasy of who and how a partner should be. When it does (and that can be a verrry long when), we get on with the business of struggling to love the person we've got.

Whether or not you were successful at that daunting emotional challenge, it's behind you now. For some of us, at the very moment of getting naked again, that old romantic daydream comes rushing back. Frankly, it can be hard to avoid, because it is swept in on a tide of fear.

Claire speaks. "I started back to dating with a terror of ending up alone. It was a financial terror because my alimony would run out someday, but it was also a fear like—who would bring me tea, for God's sake, if I broke my leg? Always, rearing its needy little head in my fantasies, was the Cinderella thing, the idea of someone to rescue me and then I wouldn't have to sell real estate. I mean, I could if I wanted to, but I wouldn't *have to*. I brought that frantic neediness to every date and I made some big messes early on because of it."

Claire has connected the two live emotional wires that might be sparking your own anxiety: the girlhood Cinderella wish for the prince ignites against a deeper dynamic concern, namely the fear of being alone.

Certainly, not every woman seeks a prince to stand guard against the werewolves of the night. We don't all rise from the ashes of a past relationship with the fantasy that a new man will step into the center of our lives and heal the pain. In fact, at the other extreme, many women vow never to open that center again, insisting on a passionate independence that precludes romantic compromise. Such a woman is apt to think of Cinderella as pathetic, especially if she recognizes her younger self in the role. She is adamant that there is no prince, though there may be plenty of men who believe they merit princely treatment.

Very often this passionately independent woman is indifferent to dating at all. That's her right, and yours. But many women who are contemplating getting naked again still find themselves in this reserved, reluctant group. If Cinderella's fear of being alone creates distorting dreams of a man who will heal all, this more cynical and defensive stepsister is dating with a chip of fear on her shoulder too. She is afraid of being trapped in a mistake.

Two Fears

Getting naked again involves many levels of play, from the frivolous (finding a discreet way to remove the cleavage cupcakes before removing the blouse) through the factual (revealing a vaginal history for the purposes of reassuring a prospective partner) and so much more. At its deepest psychodynamic level, though, getting naked again involves fear.

Of course there are an infinite number of idiosyncratic fears to bring to any new romantic encounter: the risk of making a fool of yourself or of hurting a perfectly decent person, of getting stuck with a check or bored to insanity by the dull or stalked by the obsessed, or insulted by the cruel or rejected by anyone at all. All these fears and any number of others are apt to hold emotional sway, just as the fantasies we've discussed sneak in to shape your hopes.

Beyond the buffet of common negative thoughts from which you might be sampling, you are also likely to be driven by one of two core fears these days:

- You have a fear of being alone.
- You have a fear of making a mistake.

Fear here refers to a strong unpleasant reaction—in thought or feeling—to an imagined or actual situation. Fear of being alone, for example, is a negative emotional response to being on your own, either literally (you are uncomfortable or just plain unhappy if you are even alone in the apartment) or figuratively (you can spend plenty of time on your own, as long as you are in a relationship). Your fear doesn't necessarily trigger anything as extreme as panic attacks or deep depression, though it well might. But living alone, sleeping alone, or simply having no companion might leave you with a heavy heart, a bleak mood, or the overwhelming feeling of an empty life. That heaviness, that lonely agitation churns at the prospect of spending another long, hollow weekend in only your own company or the company of your female friends. You feel a press to connect, connect, connect. Your driven behavior suggests a fear of being alone.

Fear of making a mistake, by contrast, is the set of negative thoughts and feelings that flood when the possibility of connection is upon you. In theory and on a clear, conscious level, you believe that you would like to meet the right person and enjoy a romantic relationship. But when the possibility presents itself in actuality, you find yourself recoiling. It's a fear that can rear its head anywhere along the line, from the earliest moments of interest expressed by a new acquaintance (*"Oh God. He's looking at me. Please don't let him ask for a date."*) to the very last moment of commitment paralysis, as with those who manage to get engaged but can't bring themselves to set a date.

Remember, these fears show themselves in patterns of response, not occasional occurrences. Some men will always cause you to recoil when they show interest; but when most possible lovers stir discomfort, it suggests something about you rather than about them. Similarly, some amount of alcoholic flirtation with a stranger is pain medication in itself—a reminder that there's life after loss. Frequent alcoholic hookups with strangers are a concern, both for your health and for your heart.

Of course we all feel a bit of both fears, but most likely one of these core concerns dominates. These two fears tend to fuel distinctly different romantic game plans, though you may not have known you had a plan at all. You are acting unconsciously, automatically, soothing an anxiety of which you may be only dimly conscious. But it's there. And it's influencing your behavior.

Each fear is soothed by two distinct patterns of behavior, influencing two different patterns of romantic decision making. Neither of these patterns is healthier or more dysfunctional than the other. But a mild version of the fear is better than a moderate drive; and an intense version will pretty much mean that your fear is running your show.

The intensity of your own core fear will certainly vary with your mood and/or life circumstances. For example, when your youngest child leaves for college, you might be overwhelmed by the fear of being alone; when the first grandchild comes, that same fear might ebb. Either experience could affect your romantic choices. It's not logical, but you might be influenced anyway.

Similarly, a pre-nup, separate bank accounts, even separate apartments may ease your fear of making a mistake. They won't really protect against the emotional costs of the next bad relationship—but they can lower your fear enough to have one in the first place.

You might identify your fears quite consciously, as Claire did, or you might be utterly oblivious to your own dynamics. Your behavior, though, will be a tip-off.

People driven by the fear of being alone tend to:

- Have high dependency and security needs.
- Be most vulnerable to separation issues. You probably remember struggling with homesickness as a child; you might feel pangs of sadness when you say good night after a great date; you are drawn to men who come on strong, call frequently, and appear to attach quickly. Steady but slooow feels to you like distant and uninterested.
- Hook up sexually more frequently, using alcohol to lubricate the slide into bed with a stranger.
- Assume a spirited *why not, let's party* attitude when you socialize. You are able to be upbeat, warm, and easy to engage.
- Spiral into a premature commitment, struggling to make dates into relationships and tentative relationships into marriages.
- Fall in love more easily and idealize potential partners more readily. From the fantasy pedestal on which you installed your last cute date, the fall to reality will be swift, painful, and destructive.
- Stay in a new, unsatisfying relationship long past the moment when you see its realistic limits. You substitute fantasy for satisfaction.

The intensity of your fear makes all the difference in how well or poorly it works in your life. In its mildest form, the fear of being alone opens you in a positive way to connection, and then to a new attachment. You are able to trust a new person and to express affection relatively comfortably, even though you've been hurt. Your appreciation of companionship and secure commitment make the sacrifices of any relationship easier for you to endure. You know being part of a couple costs, and you are more willing than many to pay that price.

In its extreme version, the fear of being alone can turn you from a responsible adult and mother into a full-on acting-out teenager. It's scary for a family when this happens and scarier still when it happens to you, because you may only dimly realize it.

This extreme is not just a matter of a return to mini skirts and high heels, which might evoke your children's disapproval but does them little harm. Sometimes the fear of being alone is so acute that it will drive you out into the night, blindly abandoning the family responsibilities to which you have been faithfully yoked for years. You're late for the birthday celebration because you have trouble tearing yourself away from a flirtation. You stop coming home at night, deciding the kids who still live with you are plenty old enough to be home by themselves. (Perhaps that's true, but a mom who doesn't come home *matters*.) You break babysitting dates with your grandchildren, or bring along men you've recently met and can't understand why your grown daughter would object.

If your family, and especially if your ex, confronts you regarding this new behavior, you are likely to be angry and defensive. After what he did! After what you've suffered! Isn't it your turn? Frankly, yes, it is. But your turn won't turn out right if you can't tame that tormenting fear.

Bringing that fear into consciousness and then making rational decisions about your choices is the best way to contain the effects of a driving anxiety. Claire, who recognized her own dependency fantasies, described her technique:

"The fear didn't exactly go away, but I finally learned how to handle it differently. Now when the Cinderella rescue fantasy comes up in my mind, I try to meditate it away. I just recognize it in my consciousness, feel whatever I'm feeling about fear or loss or that empty nest, and then let it go. It's like when you crave a chocolate bar but you're on a diet. The fantasy comes up, you have to notice it, recognize the pattern, and then let it float away. Once I get past my own craving, I can pay attention to the man across the table and see how I might actually feel about him."

When you notice that your own intense fear of being alone is driving you into the danger zone, you would be wise to take steps to manage it. You might

—meditate, exercise, or pray to soothe the anxiety.

—take a roommate to ease your loneliness.

—crowd your leisure time with community service.

—write yourself a list of unbreakable rules (for example, setting yourself a one-drink limit, giving yourself a safe social curfew, or setting a sleep-at-home-when-the-kids-are-home-from-college rule) to use as safety bumpers for your impulses.

It's not abnormal or weak to dread loneliness or isolation. But it can be destructive to let that dread make your decisions for you.

The fear of making a mistake has just the opposite effect. The fear of being alone overheats your blood, stirring passion where there might normally be only mild interest. By contrast, the fear of making a mistake is an icy chill that can blanket any incipient emotional warmth.

People who fear making a mistake tend to:

- Have high control needs.
- Be most vulnerable to attachment and trust issues. You are always a bit suspicious, waiting for the other shoe to drop, wondering about a new person's agenda; you try to focus on yourself, your own interests, and your own development, frequently reminding yourself not to rely on anyone.
- Be turned off by someone who is obviously interested in them.
- Arrange their physical space and/or their schedule so that there is no real opening for another person.
- Recognize a sense of relief when they realize a relationship will not "work out."
- Assume a more reserved let's-wait-and-see attitude when they begin to date.
- Move from person to person, losing interest after a predictable period of time (three or four months for some, six to seven months for many others), cataloging the deficiencies of each new prospect.
- Have long connections with partners who are (by your own determination) unsuitable or unavailable for committed relationships. Wrong age, wrong race, wrong social class, wrong location will all work well to protect you from another long-term mistake, while providing temporary companionship.
- Become serial monogamists, who take each relationship just so far and tread water until the partner, wanting more, gives up in defeat.

In its mildest form the fear of making a mistake can actually keep you from making one, and that is an enormous benefit. You are more apt to put your own life together before you seek out a partner, and that will make you a stronger and less needy partner when you do reengage.

But at the extreme it can also make you a less loving one.

An extreme fear of making a mistake will sabotage any meaningful relationship, because the only way to prevent a mistake is to refuse any emotional risk. Love, for you now, is like a great stock you put on your watch list, but you just can't bring yourself to buy. Eventually—you miss your chance. Similarly, if a loving partner comes along, you'll miss him.

You risk becoming extremely self-absorbed too, because you will be especially focused on what you want and what you need, so you can be sure you don't compromise too much. Self-sufficient is an asset; self-absorbed is a spiritual restriction. Your fear of making a mistake might make it hard to tell the difference.

Like the fear of being alone, the fear of making a mistake needs to be managed or it will become the steel emotional bars behind which you live out your life. You'll be safe there, but love is on the other side of the bars.

If your fear of making a mistake is at the extreme, reduce it by

—turning your gaze inward. If you are still focused on the flaws of each succeeding partner, you are missing the point. Your relationship paralysis has less to do with a partner's flaws (real though they are—you have a gift for spotting a lover's weaknesses) and more to do with your own anxiety.
—talking to someone about yourself and your anxiety. The fear of romantic risk is a very apt subject for psychotherapy, and this might be your moment for self-exploration.

—examining concrete relationship solutions that ease your fears. Do you need to live together first? Agree on a prenup? Negotiate written solutions to your ongoing areas of conflict?

—enumerating other life risks you've managed and noticing their outcomes. An appreciation for the potential rewards of a commitment can anchor floating fear in a realistic appreciation of love.

Here's the tricky nuance: Core fears—whether of being alone or of making a mistake—can appear as clear decisions. Why shouldn't you decide that, rather than getting trapped in another mistaken marriage and having to endure the hell of yet another divorce, you will simply never again make a commitment? Or, knowing yourself well enough to recognize that you don't thrive on your own, why shouldn't you seek committed companionship wherever you can find it? In both cases, these are rational choices well within the purview of reasonable and self-aware adults.

After all, your current boyfriend might sulk because you don't want to live with him, but that doesn't make you wrong for preferring independence. Or your lover may resent your desire for more intimacy and commitment, but wanting partnership rather than a solo life doesn't necessarily make you weak and clingy. What then is the difference between fear-driven behavior and self-aware decision making?

In the end the difference is defined by the extremes to which your fear drives you, and the consciousness with which your decisions are made. Once you tune in below your own surface, as you pay close attention to the thoughts that preoccupy you and to the choices you find yourself making, over and over, you'll be able to spot the role that fear or fantasy plays in your decision making.

We all have our own brand of fear at the core, hope as an icing, with sprinkles of anxiety and anticipation. We resume romantic life toting all this and more. It's baggage, for sure, but it's also ballast. Given this temporary confusion, wide-eyed is the happiest way to move forward. To get there, you only need to stash your agenda and open your mind.

High Heels and an Attitude

Here's a proposal for an alternative to the traditional "Know what you want, you'll be more likely to get it" advice. Instead, try on a romantic mind-set that is completely open to experience. Then see what you learn from it about yourself, about men, about sex, love, dating, and their peculiarities in middle age. It's another education.

You know how a pitcher throws a hundred balls just to warm up his arm? Have you noticed how an ice skater marks her turns in practice, just to see whether that weak ankle is still giving her trouble? Champions pay careful attention to their own mind and body responses—stretching, focusing, and working up to full strength before they throw themselves into an important game. Give yourself that same time to warm up, to pay attention to your reactions, and to practice. You will get your head back into the game at a much higher level.

Approach a man, a date, a party, a trip, thinking, "I am not seeking anything other than the experience I might have with you, here this evening. I have no agenda other than discovering what it feels like to be with you, to be in your company, to enjoy this evening, this day. Since there is nothing more that I want or need, I'm free to show you who I am, what I think, and, if I choose, how I feel. That should be interesting.

"During the course of that dinner or later, should I wish to continue the experience, I will probably try to charm you, befriend you, or even seduce you, because these are the pleasantries of courtship and I'm trying to get better at them. I might also enjoy being charmed or even seduced by you, because I'll learn something from you, and besides, it's fun.

"While we enjoy being together, we are under no emotional obligation beyond treating each other with warmth, appreciation, and courtesy. There is no expectation of putting each other first or of emotional exclusivity (though we might make sexual exclusivity part of our agreement for reasons of health, social anxiety, or moral stricture)."

This thinking is a mind shift to a here-and-now attitude, with no eye toward "Am I wasting my time? Is this person appropriate, the right age, religion, income, and all the other blah blahs of courtship?" You are focused strictly on "Does this feel good? Do I like myself here? Is there something I can find to like about this other person? Is there something I can learn? Is there a risk I might want to venture, just for the hell of it? How good can I be? How bad can I get away with being, just for the hell of it?"

Believe me, there will be plenty of time later to worry about all the traditional preoccupations of courtship: "Is he the one? Is he commitment-phobic? Can he be trusted? Does he drink, smoke, cheat, gamble, steal, or have some other catastrophic flaw? Can he handle a relationship, tolerate being close, talk about feelings, tell the truth? Is he too spoiled, self-absorbed, cheap, mean, lazy, or jealous to bother with? Does he have any money? Does he love me? Do I love him? And, if I throw my lot in with him, exactly how many tantrums or episodes of road rage will I have to endure?"

All of these and more of the inescapable female concerns of love are still in the offing for you. You won't have to do without them forever. But these are relationship concerns, and I am suggesting that you hold off on all those where-is-this-relationship-going? themes for a period of time. Just long enough to get good at courtship again, to see the process clearly, and to find pleasure in it. After all, the more comfortable you are, the less likely you are to rush into a relationship just to get dating out of the way.

For a woman tentatively getting naked again, the benefits of this philosophy are obvious. For one thing, if you still have kids at home, it's an attitude that allows you to have a man or men in your life without threatening your primary focus on the well-being of your children. We all know how easy it is to lose ourselves in a rush of romantic fantasy. Next thing you know, Ariel-home-from-college is meeting a nice man in a bathrobe over her morning Cheerios. Sure, she's seen it with her roommate. But frankly, Mom is an entirely different story.

Even if your kids have long outgrown your breakfast table, you can still benefit from this philosophy of independence. It's an attitude that will help you to develop necessary adult companionship without trying to transform that into a serious relationship by the alchemy of emotional hunger. It leaves you open to meeting and dating people who might, in the long run, make more suitable life companions.

The purpose of this here-and-now mind shift is to give yourself a period of time for slow reentry into courtship and love. It's time you'll use to reawaken the flirt that got buried beneath the twenty extra pounds marriage added to your spirit. Time to play and maybe walk away before the next attachment puts you right back in the compromise and struggle of relationship building. It's time to sort out and stabilize your kids, learn how to manage your money, build your own professional relationship with an insurance agent and a plumber.

It will also increase your ability to take a romantic risk. This mind shift is a philosophy of transition. Its purpose is quite simple: *to break through your emotional ice.* It opens you to make a call, take the risk, do the asking or even the kissing—to try any of the courtship moves that make all of us anxious at first. You are more apt to try them when the stakes are lower, and once you try them—they get easier.

Perhaps most useful of all, a here-and-now, no-agenda approach gives you time to rediscover men and to come to a more peaceful acceptance of the fact that they are, in fact, not women. They do not offer the same conversation as women, the same companionship as women, the same intuitive emotional response as women. They are, first and foremost, male, and this means they are generally tuned to a different frequency.

Over the course of your last long relationship it was all too easy to forget these inherent gender differences because you put in a thousand hours of conversation and confrontation in order to bridge them. Too, all men are not alike, and any individual male (or female, for that matter) is likely to vary wildly from a stereotypic gender characterization. There is certainly a continuum in the men you will encounter—say, from the metrosexual to the animal sexual—and their interests, communication skills, and all-around awareness of the female psyche will be different from person to person.

Still, dating returns us to the land of the generic male, at least until the surface is penetrated and a connection is established. (And in some areas, way longer than that.) You've gotta learn to love that guy thing or dating will be a circle of hell.

A here-and-now attitude, with less emotional investment in the future, gives you a real opportunity to relax and accept a man for what he is, rather than holding out for what—in your opinion—he should be, or for what you are entitled to. The first time you can avoid taking something he does personally, the first time you think, "Oh, that's just how men are," instead of overanalyzing some small piece of behavior, you have the payoff of your new attitude. That alone makes it worth striving for.

Even with these benefits though, wrenching your emotional focus away from the goal of finding love and toward an appreciation of the moment is huge and hard. Shifting focus goes against our social training and more—it sometimes fights against our unbidden but overwhelming emotional need. Your stubborn, injured, shaky heart wants something, hopes for something far beyond this one drink.

Well, maybe so. Emotional longings might make a here-and-now attitude a distant star. Still, it's worth trying for. Your heart feels what it feels; we can't change that. But even if you don't achieve this stage of sweet equanimity in dating, it's worth the effort to visit the neighborhood. An iota more openness in your attitude pays off in interesting experience.

Women who have been able to make the shift from "Where is

this going?" to "Let me try this on" reported using some mental tricks to make the shift:

> I looked on every date as a dinner party, where you are expected to make interesting conversation with the person next to you, even though you will probably never see that person again in your life. That attitude gave me some wonderful evenings, with some unlikely people. It all ended up making me feel better about being desirable.

> I decided that I just wanted to go out. I didn't like that being single gave me fewer choices, but it did. So I just said yes to wherever I was asked. That got me more places and eventually better invitations.

> I make it clear that I'm just having fun, and men like that a lot. Single women ask me, "How are you meeting men who take you out?" I don't want to tell them, but I'm thinking, "You have on three inches of makeup, you are wearing a shit pile of jewelry, you have four-inch nails. You are advertising on some Web site with a cringey little saying like 'Be my first mate.' You are just trying waaaay too hard, and it smells desperate."

Try whatever trick of the mind or makeup works for you to relax your requirements and your spine and open up to experience. It won't be comfortable in the beginning, but dating too gets easier with practice. You're rusty right now. If you've been long married, or mired in motherhood, or so corporate that your lingerie never shows (or so long in the sexual coma that you don't own anything that could remotely be called lingerie), it's not so easy to slip into heels and remember to ask him about himself. If you want to get good at it again, you'll need practice. Understand that during this time you are expanding your own comfort level. In that way

—every coffee meeting with a computer date who turns out
    to have lied about his age and his hair,
—every potential lover who can't quite manage an erection and
    suggests that you help him more than you'd rather,
—every singles event you attend that sets you back to your
    bad prom days,
—every dance, dinner, or concert invitation you extend
    that gets turned down flat by a man who wasn't nearly
    good enough for you in the first place, only he doesn't
    know it,

is simply basic training. Over time, surviving bad experiences, appreciating the good ones, you will become more relaxed, more flirtatious, more available for connection. If you let yourself, that is. If you don't get crazy and isolated and muttering aloud about the weaknesses of men and the hopelessness of affection. Reducing this hazardous outcome is one major reward of this here-and-now mind shift.

A *let's try this on* attitude also provides a small shield against the tendency of some women to fling themselves over the cliff into love at their first orgasm. When you've been numb for some time—congealed in bad marriage endurance mode, stuck in the emotionless drudgery of professional success, lost in the sudden desert of widowhood—almost any rush of feeling for another person can be confused with love.

Throw in the female foible of enjoying sex more when a partner is beloved, add the urge to re-create a secure harbor as shelter from the loneliness of being Back Out There, and it's easy to confuse sexual passion with lifetime partnership. That's how you end up with bad second marriages, patterns of abusive relationships, and blended families that no sane person would ever attempt to fold together.

A mind-set that deliberately resists an agenda can be an antidote for these emotional vulnerabilities. However high your tides of passion run, however tapped out may be your energy for the game, your goal right now is simply experience itself. You can avoid the shoals of either commitment or retreat until you are wise enough to make those judgments from a stable and strong position. Stable and strong occurs only

—over time,
—with experience,
—after you've taken some risks,
—and survived to laugh about them,

assuming you can convince yourself it's worth the bother.

Why Not Sit This One Out?

You get to an age where you don't want anything you have to feed or water.

—Ann Richards

"I don't want to play," you might say. "I'm tired of the game, pained by the game, maybe even still bleeding from my last toss of the dice. I'd be interested in love if it came along, love and genuine feeling—but I certainly don't want sex without that gauzy glow. It's not fun, it's not hot, and it's not even moral. Plus, I'm sick of falsehood and pretense, and way too old to laugh at those long jokes with punch lines that men tell endlessly and expectantly. I'm just not gonna laugh at another one of those."

For these and other good reasons, an awful lot of us are going to sit this one out. Forever. We convince ourselves to do so for three powerful reasons:

- We disqualify ourselves.
- We discount men.
- We savor newly acquired freedom.

Your own stew of feelings might include all three.

Disqualifying yourself is chillingly easy. After all, dating and menopause are not natural cohorts. To find them overlapping in your life could be considered God's joke. The very idea of practicing deep-throating a banana with post-menopausal zest might be considered sillier still. It's inevitable, then, that you will begin a bad-news broadcast in your head—the one that regularly telegraphs "*too old, too fat, too tired*" every time you consider turning up at your church Senior Singles Social.

And that description doesn't just cover the people you anticipate meeting. That's you you're talking about—and you are talking yourself back onto your couch.

Are you too old, too fat, or just too exhausted to get back into the game? Well, on some days you are. On some days even Christie

Brinkley is, I betcha—and she's just unexpectedly turned single too. (Talk about your competition . . .)

Basically —too old, too fat, and too tired are the three mental demons that must be confronted and countered if you are going to even take a step in a playful direction. Remember, it could be only a step, a small risk, a toe in the water, a smile at a stranger, a party alone, the movie buffs club without the movie buff who used to go with you, one trip with the ski club because at the very least you'll get to ski. Only a step . . . and then the next one.

First you'll have to step past the thought "I'm too tired." If you're tired tonight, fine—take the night off. You don't have to be out out out, just because you're single. Put your feet up and veg. If you are "too tired" all the time, well, that's another story. See your doctor and figure out whether you have a physical problem. If you don't, that fatigue is depression, emotional exhaustion, or a combination of the two. You need some help—counseling, meds, the support of friends—to get your engine to turn over. Chronically too tired or too overwhelmed to play is a quiet crisis. Pay attention.

Too fat—wow, there's a showstopper. It has just enough truth to be impossible to dismiss and just enough nutsiness to become the iron curtain behind which you hide forever.

I don't know whether you are, in fact, too fat to date. Check your BMI for an objective read. If you score in the obesity range, your biggest concern is the serious health risk you are ignoring. I've spent my share of time in this battle, and I know it's an awful place. Use your dating desire as motivation to take on the cruel struggle of eating management, reduce your weight by even 10 percent, and you will have given yourself a fantastic health and energy gift—plus you are more likely to have sex again before you die. Even if you, like many of us, consider sex and cheese-cake about an even trade, it's so great to feel proud of yourself again that it's worth it.

For most of us, the question of being too fat for dating is largely subjective. Are you at your ideal weight? Maybe not, but a quick scan of people holding hands at the mall will show you that being fat does not exclude people from dating. *Feeling* too fat, however, does.

There's an edge a woman requires to build the confidence to flirt. Its source is mysterious—some combination of sexual hormone surge, past positive male response, and a truly great haircut. Whatever gives you that swagger, five extra pounds are likely to squelch it. This is not natural, reasonable, or sane. But, for many women, it is the case. So—if you are *feeling* too fat to date, take off those few pounds that get in the way of your walk.

Be careful, though, not to hide out in a diet. Take off those first pounds of bloat and then get out there. It's so easy to decide that you need to lose the thirty or the fifty before you qualify for a fix-up. Then, either you never quite achieve your goal or you get skinny and anxious, have two tortured blind dates, and re-treat to Dunkin' Donuts for solace. Back come the thirty pounds plus a few new ones, and in the meanwhile, time you don't have is passing you by.

Conclusion: Get back on a healthier eating and workout path for a few weeks (yeah, yeah, I know it should be forever . . .) and let the increased possibility of dating and romance be your trade-off for cozy nights in bed with chocolate chip cookies. But do not use *too fat* as your rationalization for retreat. Instead, recog-nize that you're anxious—who isn't—and cut the scary romance steps into bite-size pieces. (In part II you'll find some suggestions for you.)

Finally, foremost, the killer—"*I'm too old for this.*" Not so long ago, you would certainly have been right. Was it only three generations ago that a woman of sixty or so would lose her husband and nest into grandchildren and good works? Now she plumps her lips, presses weights, and considers silicone implants—while babysitting and doing good works, of course. (We always seem to add to our list. We are not great at editing.)

The only point is that *too old* for romantic enterprise is self-defined. In fact, as compared with the traditional courtship period of one's twenties, older women have a few distinct advantages in the game. (Okay, okay—just a few. But don't ignore the aces in the hand.)

For one thing, you don't have to take romance so seriously. You aren't building your nest (though you may be looking to feather it). However much we dress up dating in our twenties as a fun and sexy activity involving shoes, it has a serious underlying purpose. We are seeking stable fathers for our children, and biology has placed us on a timetable. A grim sense of urgency and wrenching vulnerability underlies many blind dates and bar hookups.

You are now back in the twenty-something game, but without the biological baggage you carried. Plus, you care less about what other people think, and that means you can reveal more of yourself than you ever did when you were dating before. You can be funnier, less inhibited, more opinionated, more yourself. Your increased confidence and authenticity make romantic life more relaxed this time around, if you let them.

You are smarter now too, and more knowledgeable about

people. This is as close as we come to realizing the common dream of being twenty again, but with the benefit of all we've learned along the way. You will be more likely to savor this experience, of course, if you can muster even a little of that here-and-now attitude. And you will, as you learn to get your head into the game.

Discounting available men, along with disqualifying yourself, is another rationale for sitting this one out. You will say that there are no men, or at least no quality ones. You will note that the odds of meeting that one good man are against you, that you are too old in male eyes, and frankly plenty of them look too old to you. You may endure an online match or two, decide that the whole thing is not worth bothering with, and settle in with a bowl of mint chocolate chip ice cream and another episode of *Law & Order.* What's the point?

"There's a disconnect," one woman explained. "I only find the sexiness, the sizzle, with men ten to fifteen years younger than me, and men my age feel the same about me. I get around a lot, travel, sit on boards, meet lots of men. But I feel like I'm not arm candy enough for them." This particular sixty-three-year-old is arm candy enough for the married man with whom she has been having a sexually hot, though infrequently scheduled affair for the last two years, so some might find her dating angst less moving. Still, her point of view is common enough to note.

Aging brains and bodies are sexually abhorrent to many men and women. (Of course, this means that those of us with a taste for older men have the field wide open.) Certainly both men and women have an appetite for relative youth. (*Relative* being the operative word at this point. Single at fifty in LA might well feel invisible. Get on a plane and fly to Palm Beach and you will get off the plane a sex object. It's something to think about.)

And it's true that, Demi Moore notwithstanding, men seem to get more opportunity to gratify that taste for youth than most women do. You might be bitter about this inequity, or you might accept it philosophically as the way of the world. Either way, your distaste for an aging partner or discomfort with your own age could keep you out of the game if you let it.

Some women believe that as long as they are wearing a smile, a new lover shouldn't have a problem. But you may be one of those who has a heartfelt conviction that no man will want you once he sees you without the bra. One widow expressed her reluctance perfectly. "When you grow old with someone, you grow accustomed to his aging body and he to yours. The idea of having to look at a strange naked old man, or having him see me—it's horrifying." Well, at the very least it argues for many more trips to the gym than you may be inclined to make.

As single adults we are sensitive to our precarious status in the couples world in which we all live, but that doesn't keep any of us from judging other single people with remarkable harshness. "I don't go online anymore," one woman explained, "because frankly everyone I met was a retread or a loser. The good ones get snapped up right away and the rest are left over for a reason."

Certainly you are free to indulge in as much ruthless judgment as is your bent, but

—if you confine your romantic inclinations to those who have maintained the coiffure or abdominals of their younger days,

—if you make a clear-eyed assessment of a date's financial viability but resent the way he appraises your own net worth,

—if you are suspicious of the long divorced because he will probably never remarry,

—and nervous around the newly divorced because he isn't ready yet,

—and wary of the widower who won't let go of his old life to make room for you,

—if you are searching each new prospect to identify his flaw, so you can protect yourself from it, then

just be aware that you are, in effect, sitting this one out. Every individual acid evaluation might be perfectly apt, but you might also be missing an interesting time. Those men you have discounted as old guys or losers or boring or bratty may be all those things. But if you aren't necessarily looking to marry one of them, you can sample from their strengths and set the weaknesses aside. Or you can sideline yourself. Your call.

Finally, and with passion, **freedom itself** might be your strongest reason for sitting this one out. If that's your driving need, you'll prefer your romance with built-in steel boundaries.

There is a freedom that can only come from not being part of a couple, a freedom to meet only your own expectations and wash only your own underwear. It's the freedom to leave the TV on as late as you want, or turn the damn thing off and never overhear another March Madness game as long as you live. Live without a man, without a relationship, and you live with the simple pleasure of enjoying your favorite cold cereal for dinner without having to serve up whole wheat pasta for your cholesterol-obsessed spouse. It's the divine freedom—more commonly associated with men, whether married or not—to put yourself first, middle, and last. Only a rare wife and mother is able simply to suit herself much of the time.

The fresh experience of pleasing yourself may make the prospect of a new relationship positively punishment. Women are a marching army of Pleasers, trained from our earliest days to find the way to his heart through his stomach, and then through a highly personalized massage. We provide meals and clean clothes and Christmas traditions and frequently half the income too, plus children of whom he can be proud, and an established network of people he can call "family" though he has rarely been known to call them without prompting.

True, we've been so pissed off about having to do all of this that few of our men end up all that pleased to be around us, which is one reason we ended up single again in the first place. (Just one of the reasons, but still, something that bears remembering.) The point is, we have aimed to please, and it's an amazing thing to have no one left to please but me, myself, and I.

One friend, Rosa, tried to explain what she unexpectedly celebrated in the divorce she did not seek. "I'm a caretaker—it's who I am. And in my marriage I always did what he wanted me to do because, frankly, him being happy was the most important thing to me. The whole time, he was tough—moody, difficult to satisfy. I didn't even know it then, but I was always on edge trying to make him happy. Now I'm so relaxed, so free. I'm soaring like an eagle and I never knew I had that in me. Why would I date? I think I'm dating the greatest girl, and that's me!"

Ask Marlene, widowed after forty years of marriage, if she

wants to date, and she has a ready list of what she'd have to give up: "What if I have a boyfriend who sleeps on my side of the bed? Or he likes the heat too high or he cringes over the air-conditioning bill? What if he dislikes my business or he roots against my team? A long-term marriage is like a choreographed dance where you learn to move together and appreciate the same things. I just can't imagine putting up with a whole new set of accommodations."

Marlene is single, satisfied, and passionate about the interior design business she developed in the last few years of her husband's life. But she does speak frankly about the way she restricts herself to those few avenues where she's comfortable alone. "I travel alone for business all the time and I love it. But I wouldn't go to a resort alone, or take a vacation alone. I don't even go into restaurants alone, because it's just too lonely for me. I miss my husband then. I think my life is extremely exciting and exhilarating, but I do avoid the social world where it's all couples. Maybe I'm just too nervous to date. If someone found the perfect guy for me, and they knew the man very well, I'd be open to a relationship. But you know, I just can't picture myself seeking it out."

There's that core resistance, that emotional obstacle with which you too may wrestle. Companionship, not to mention partnership, is still desirable. But the sheer effort required to get online, slip back into high heels, coordinate orgasms, meet someone else's chilly sons or possessive daughters, figure out if he's willing to eat Indian food or he's read anything past *The Da Vinci Code*, the overwhelming *work* of relationships, would nudge even hardy and highly sexual spirits toward those comforting three G's of later life: Grandchildren, Gardening, and God.

Even the most optimistic among us finds romantic reentry

daunting. For one thing, you feel utterly on your own. It's you on that date, at that bar, in that bedroom. You—feeling judged, vulnerable, inadequate. You—opening again to romance and then suffering the heart pangs of disappointment, longing, or frustration that are the shadow side of dating cheer. Knowing all this, feeling all this, some nights everything in you signals: Quit. Go home and feed your orchid plants. And here I am saying, "Stay out there. Here—let me show you how." Before we get to how, it helps to know why it's worth the bother.

Sex, Love, and Social Chitchat

Should you bother returning to romance because life without sex is not worth living? No, if that were the case no one would stay married, since we all know that, besides motherhood, few experiences sap sexual energy more reliably than marriage. (And most of us combine marriage with motherhood—the true erotic hemlock.) But life is better with fun sex, and one of the great advantages of being single is that you can actually escape having obligatory married sex and try some fun sex. There are so many downsides to being single, it seems a shame to miss out on the one great plus.

And yes, there are men, functional normal men, who will want to have sex with you—even though you are fifty or sixty or even, occasionally, eighty, frankly. They will want to have sex with you because they like sex and so do you, because they enjoy your company and sex is a natural extension of that company, because you make a memorable lemon chiffon pie, because they think they might learn to love you, because you are *not* forty and therefore not a threat to become pregnant and saddle them with a whole new family when all they were looking for was a later-in-life companion.

Some men will want to have sex with you because they'd like to get closer to you and sex is the only route they know, because you remember the same songs, share the same politics, and sometimes because you don't mind picking up the check. And maybe because, whatever your age, you're sexually attractive and so, why wouldn't he want to?

And you might want to bother having sex with him too—because skin has a hunger to be touched and another moment in someone's arms is emotionally sustaining for long past that moment. Besides, a sex life is just generally all-around good for you. It's good for your circulation and your hair and your longevity and your overall outlook. As long as you can enjoy it without getting a rash (not that difficult) or breaking your heart (trickier, but possible; see chapter 8), having a lover is a great reason to bother with the game.

You might want to experience a new lover because you are finally more comfortable with yourself sexually now, more confident, more responsive, and more willing to let a partner know what feels good. Hey—you just may just be willing finally to let yourself know what feels good after many years of keeping a watchful ear out for the kids or suppressing the thought that your husband is a fine guy but a really bad kisser. (Certainly you don't want to die without having experienced a really good kisser, do you? Well then, you must get back into the game.)

Too, if you choose to resume romantic life, the men you encounter may offer smoother and more interesting seductions than you've experienced before. The first sexual night, for example, might be staged with more thought and better reservations because he is editing from his last forty years of encounters. Plus, he is more likely to have the financial wherewithal to make those reservations, and that—if you will honestly refresh your memory of the motels, dorm rooms, and cars of your youth—is really a plus.

Surprisingly, the sex itself may also be better. Yes, it's way easier for younger men to get hard and stay hard, and they may require less from you as a result. (Prefer, certainly. But require—not usually.) Older lovers do have more mechanical problems. *But* that absence of urgent arousal often pays off in attentiveness to the female sexual response that was just not possible when he was hotter and hornier.

One seventy-year-old man described it this way: "When I was younger, my own sexual arousal completely dominated me. I didn't need a woman to be so responsive. I knew I was supposed to pay attention, but I probably didn't. Just, you know, went through the motions. A woman who is sexually responsive now has much more impact on me, so that makes me much more concerned with what she thinks and feels."

A man who is more likely to pay attention in bed is reason enough to get back into the game, if only for the novelty of the experience. For some of us, getting naked again means finally enjoying getting naked. You'll have to try it to find out if that's true for you.

And it might be true for you even if you haven't experienced driving sexual desire for some time. That wouldn't be surprising, since diminished sexual desire is a significant concern for women, whether they have partners or not. Female desire is a complicated thing, impacted as profoundly by that great sex organ, the brain, as it is by any of our other parts. We are affected by our partner's techniques, but also by his kindness, his conversation, and whether he took out the garbage like he promised.

Just because your sexuality has gone underground, and especially if you don't have a ready partner, don't feel you have to abandon it entirely. There is, to date, no female Viagra. But you will benefit from having a physician you can talk with frankly, an open attitude toward sexual aids, and a commitment to sexual health. A great sexual partner sometimes follows a healthy sexual intention.

Of course, resuming romantic life is not all about sex, though staying alive sexually is a big piece of it. It's also about being in a larger world, about connecting intellectually with some wider range of people than you would if you chose to sit this one out. It's about expressing and receiving affection and about holding open the possibility of experiencing love again. Both of those are emotional possibilities that enhance life right up to the moment of death.

At a more prosaic level, getting naked again keeps you in touch with men, and men have a tremendous amount to offer, especially if you are not caught in the struggle to get something from one of them. Keep in mind this Golden Rule: At this point in life, getting naked again is not, nor should it be, your full-time activity. It's icing, high heels, and gravy. It's functional (a man to call when dancing is on the agenda); it's flattering (a man who will tell you, when you need to hear it, that you look amazing); it's supportive (a man who cares what the biopsy says); it is potentially sexually satisfying (this really needs no explanation, unless it does, in which case you really have been away from the party too long). This list is by no means all-inclusive, but the point is that while getting naked again could satisfy a variety of needs, it was never meant to be a full-time preoccupation.

At thirty, you knew what you wanted from a man, or thought you did. Now, though, with a long relationship and parenting decisions behind you, with your financial picture developed and your personal interests, passions, quirks, and preferences evolved, it's not clear what role a man should or would play in your life. The field is open. Fools rush in.

So I'm saying, yes, take off your floral sweat suit and go back out there. But go with a lighter heart and a willingness to be surprised, especially by yourself. Go because you care less these days about what other people think of you and dating is a good place to spend that bank account of confidence. Go because it will make you laugh, teach you something, open up resources, connections, and opportunities that you can only get from new people who live in different worlds. Go because you are testing yourself and spirits grow stronger in the crucible of a test. Go because all the difficulties of adult love are out there and they are part of our point in being here. Don't miss the point.

Go back into the world of romance even though it takes energy, it hurts, you will cry, you will feel rejection, and it will have many unfunny moments. Go back, whether with your whole body or, for today, with only a smile and a risky direct gaze. But keep romance in your life for this best reason: because it is one true source of life's juice.

Call that energy spiritual, sexual, or emotional—the label doesn't matter. It's our life force, and we want to keep it glowing to the last possible second. Romantic life, in its many forms, can be one true catalyst. Go back.

And you will

—when your head is lodged firmly in *"Let's try it on,"*
—and the ten extra pounds, or gray roots, or saggy smocks
  are banished at least temporarily,
—and your spirit, while wary, is ready,

then let the games begin.

PART TWO

Interpersonal Expertise

CHAPTER FIVE

Act I: They Meet

There are no men. That's the incontrovertible, impossible romantic obstacle women face when we hope to return to romantic life. And if, in fact, there are no men, then everything else is just commentary.

We didn't make it up. If by *men* you mean

—single, socially appropriate, reasonably attractive, emotionally available, financially stable, physically fit, sexually monogamous, healthy, legally unentangled, temperamentally even, loving yet independent, reasonable, generous, smart, and, if possible, funny men

well, there are so few of those that you might as well go with none. If, on the other hand, you are willing to make an important emotional and social connection with your basic normal guy, you will have a few from whom to choose.

A man is a romantic ideal. (See above; alter description according to your own personal profile.) A guy, on the other hand, might show up wearing the wrong clothes, having an insufficient amount of capital; he might have a history of cancer or complain about his chronically bad knees way more often than you find interesting. A guy might be available only for Saturday-night dates when you were looking for a lifetime companion. Or a guy might want a woman who will bring him coffee in bed and you have been there, done that, and envision separate beds at this point in your life.

A guy might be the one you thought initially was too old for you, or the one who gets imperious with waitresses. A guy could have an unattractive gut and still be eating hot dogs, or else be obsessed with his abs and sniff with disapproval every time you have an ice cream cone. A guy is less educated than you, less successful than your ex, or less socially polished than your friends and family.

A man makes love to you and savors the experience, but a guy worries about his ability, and sometimes he has reason to worry. A man understands why your kids have to come first and he overcomes their jealous behavior with a charm offensive of his own. A guy, however, gets testy when he's always second on the list—especially if your kids force him to delay dinner, sex, or a play-off game.

If you've been back in the game for even a brief period of time, you probably have guy examples of your own. Whatever the case, you get the point: You may be right that there are no men, and those who exist are spoken for. But there are guys around—to flirt with, date, sleep with, travel with, cook for, play tennis or hike or sail with, commit to—and even to love, if you are able and willing to love a guy.

If you are resuming romantic life after a long hiatus—tucked into a marriage, for example, or buried under the avalanche of single motherhood—you may have been oblivious to the fact that romantic liaisons between people of your age and demographic are occurring all around you. It may seem to you that the whole world is coupled up already, preoccupied with college admissions, empty nests, or grandchildren, enjoying family trips to China or cozily planning retirement together.

Well, look around again. Single people (and some married ones, truth to tell) are still playing the game—playing it at forty and at seventy. Playing it at the office and in the assisted living home. Playing it poorly or well, for laughs as well as for love, and certainly playing it for money. You just didn't notice before.

The courtship game may be the only permanent floating craps game in town. There is always a game if you know where to look, though certainly as people leave their thirties (by which time the majority have partnered up for their first go-round) the play goes underground. What you need, to get into the game, are targets of opportunity. To unearth other players, you will probably have to take a risk and make an effort. Ucccch. But it's the case.

Single men and women cross paths—accidentally, deliberately, routinely, and by magnificent serendipity. When they do, presuming one or the other has the interest, the initiative, and sometimes the imagination, they send a signal. With a little luck, there's an RSVP. That's how and where you meet someone with whom to play.

For example, one fifty-one-year-old jewelry designer described an invitation to connect sent his way: "We had worked for the same company for months, but I'd never thought of her. Then she sent me a valentine, which I definitely took as a sign of possibility. I asked her for lunch and we've been dating ever since.

It wasn't until a year later that I found out she sends valentines to all her friends."

Or this sixty-seven-year-old widower who reported his response to an unfamiliarly straightforward signal: "We were in an elevator and to tell the truth, I could not stop looking at her breasts, which were presented the way you can on an elevator in Florida, but you can't in Philadelphia. Or maybe people do in Philadelphia but I didn't notice before, because I was married. Anyway, when she got off at her floor, she looked right at me and said, 'I'll be by the pool at three o'clock.' I don't know how I got the balls, I was totally ill at ease, but I felt I had to be man enough to show up. She patted the lounge chair next to her, I sat in it, and she's living with me now."

Some connections evolve slowly. A fifty-five-year-old marketing rep: "For years I've been collecting jokes and sending them to a huge e-mail list. It's my little attempt to lighten life. I met a woman on a train, we chatted, and I mentioned my joke project. She said she'd like to be on the list, so I added her name. I didn't think a thing about her, but every so often when I sent a joke, she sent one back. That began an e-mail relationship, which moved into a friendship that we've started to take further."

Other initiatives are easily misunderstood. Or, perhaps you will think, understood all too well. A sixty-three-year-old, long-divorced investment analyst tells this story: "I'm at a large party, guest of my current girlfriend, and I don't know many people there. Across the room I see a beautiful, sultry, single woman I've known over the years, and I make my way over to talk to her. We chat about this or that for a few minutes and then she asks, 'Aren't you still dating Gina?' 'Yes, I am. She's right over there.' 'So,' she said, 'what are you doing over here, hitting on me?' I left right away, but I wanted to ask her, 'What makes you such a bitch?' "

Sometimes signals are simply effective marketing ploys. A twice-divorced retired physician: "I started going to these 'business and professionals' singles dances, but I'm not very good at dancing and I'm not good-looking enough to attract much attention. Then I talked the director into having a singles cocktail party at my house. Once the women saw where I lived, they made it a point to come over and talk to me. That made it easy."

Other signs come gift-wrapped in social niceties. "I met my last girlfriend, well, remet her actually, when she had a mutual friend arrange a dinner and invite me along. She was someone I had known since I was a kid, and in those years I thought she was terrific. I guess she must have heard that I was recently single—not that my being in a relationship would have stopped her, come to think of it—but anyway, we all went out and I took it from there. I was enchanted with the woman I remembered and thought her to be. It was a good six months before I recognized her for the whack job she actually was."

And sometimes the signal that feels safest is the clear bell of availability that rings on an Internet dating site or a dating service, where the only other people to hear the chime are those sending similar messages. "I've done dating services like It's Just Lunch, and I've used the whole e-mail, online thing. You meet a lot of nice, attractive women," said one longtime-single businessman. "I could date the friends of friends, but it always feels a little too close for comfort. Eventually the friends want to know what's going on and you feel like you're letting them down. Dating services introduce me to women with whom I have no other social relationship. That privacy, to conduct my relationships without being judged, is very important to me."

Act I: They Meet. And so must you, if you intend to get back into the game. But how and where best to send your own signal? And most of all—to whom?

It's worth noting again that this is the obstacle women identify as the most daunting. "Forget it. There are no men," an accomplished, divorced high school principal flatly stated. In fact, she was alone and without even the prospect of a date for a full two years—until she met the man she married last month.

Her experience is not atypical. Whereas earlier in life it seemed that the next man was just a beer or an interesting party away, this woman felt that she emerged from her long marriage into a romantic Kalahari. "Even Moses would have cracked under my dry spell."

Her new partner is a man she met at a professional conference who maintained a warm, collegial connection for a full year before he finally—the pace was torment—came over one night with champagne. Seems he had a relationship to end before he felt quite right starting the next one. Seems there might be a man or two left worthy of loving, though the wait can be discouraging. Frankly, if love doesn't kill you, the dry spell might.

The prospect of love appears capriciously, and it's always a rare bird. But romance, courtship, dating, flirtation, sex, affection, and interesting conversation are all available along the way. You can enjoy any or all of these, if you are open to a wide variety of partners who are not necessarily prospects for love. They are practice, stimulation, and possibly even pleasant company. At the very least, they will take you a step toward getting naked again, and that's a step in the right direction.

"Fine fine fine," you're thinking. "I'm persuaded. But where are these men to whom I'm supposed to be so open? And how am I supposed to meet them?"

Gender Injustice

Let's confront one ugly truth first, just in case it's standing in your way. To meet a man might require that you put forth more effort than that same man has to put forth to meet you. This is neither fair nor just. But what is?

Every man interviewed for this book spoke about his ample opportunity to meet available women: "There are single women—attractive, cheerful, and interested in me—at nearly every party I walk into," one twice-divorced retiree mentioned. He wasn't bragging, not really. (Okay, maybe a smidge.) He was describing his experience.

Several men confided that they were overwhelmed with phone numbers of potential candidates, from the moment of separation. "I deliberately went very slowly, especially sexually," one widower explained. "I learned quickly that most women are sexually available, but just as quick to emotionally attach. I didn't want to get a reputation in my small community as some kind of cad."

Men who prefer social pre-selection are usually able to confine their dating to women recommended by friends. Single women are offered comparatively fewer introductions. Why?

Well, partly it's numbers, certainly. Men do die off faster, so there are fewer of them as we age. And partly it's pure dating demographics. We do like to date up, they do like to date down, and the bottom of the pyramid is simply wider than the top. Plus, there's the social dynamic that pairs the sexiness of youthful beauty with the protective appeal of mature wealth. This romantic exchange favors the younger woman and the older man, if only because men get their goods later and hold on to them longer. Result—they have a wider age pool of potential partners than do women of a similar age.

Are you bitter yet?

Plus, men get more introductions because women do most of the fixing up and your girlfriend likely has four or five single women friends for maybe every one eligible widower she knows. If that. And she may not even be close enough to the newly eligible male to make a suggestion to him. When or if she mentions your name, it will be one of several he has heard recently.

Wanna give up?

Strangely, though, those few men, the very ones with the dozen introductions, will tell you that there are few fit, attractive women who will be sweet and uncritical and not make them give up the hours of basketball they prefer watching, women who will continue to want to have sex with them instead of being mad all the time, women who will not make them throw away their favorite soup-stained flannel shirt. And, they would say, no matter how many women they meet, that's why they are still looking.

Just like you.

That's the thing. Men who have the opportunity to meet so many women are still trying hard to find The One. (Okay, not—say—for that first model-lust year after the divorce. But eventually.) Oddly enough, screening the many does not make that divorced guy any more likely to find his One than struggling to meet the few does for you. It's all about making a connection, experiencing a click, and going from there.

So the competition doesn't have to scare you. It's just a fact of life that might encourage you to extend yourself a bit further outside your comfort zone. He's looking for you, and he has women to sort through. So be it. You'll need to help him find you, that's all.

Women who get comfortable enough with romantic life to take a few risks do find partners with whom to play. They find these partners at age fifty and at sixty-five and later too. They remarry, or remate, live alone or together, travel together or separately, make love, and sometimes break up and start again.

True, these women are apt to have long empty spells, when their male counterparts have an easier time filling the space— should they choose to—with escorts, pleasant or irritating dates, casual sexual partners, and various other placeholders of the heart. But in the end, both men and women of every age find partners for the game who offer them pleasure, companionship, and occasionally love. Stay in long enough and you will too, I betcha.

But how? Where?

Single adults connect with each other

—by taking a second, sexual look at their social network themselves,

—by extending that social network into likely new territory, and

—by deliberately asking that social network to do some looking for them.

You might need to try all three. Start with the last, because it can never hurt.

Asking your social network—friends, family, colleagues—to do some looking for you is awkward, but it gets more results than not asking. Asking means letting your friends know that you are open to meeting men, that you'd love them to keep you in mind if they are thinking of introducing a friend to someone.

For many of us this simple, open, cheerful request is humiliation akin to realizing that your skirt got caught in your underpants and stayed there for the whole rest of the party. Make it easier by practicing a few lines. When a friend or acquaintance gives you an opening (by saying, "Are you seeing anyone?" or "What's new lately?"), try one of these responses:

"You know what I'd enjoy? If you're ever introducing people, keep me in mind. I'm interested in adding new people to my life right now."

Or, "I've been fixed up several times and that's been a great way to meet people. I'm open to that happening more often."

Or, most productive of all, mention some specific trait, because it gives your friends a useful introductory hook. "I'd love to meet a new tennis partner . . . salsa dancer . . . travel buddy . . . wine appreciator . . . art collector . . . flea-market buff . . . opera lover . . ." Fill in the blank with any and every activity that might trigger the thought processes of your acquaintance.

That connective hook makes it easier for your friend to make an introduction. "I have a girlfriend who wants to visit Tibet, and I know you traveled there last year. Could I arrange for you two to have a drink together?" is a far more comfortable entrée than, "I have a nice friend. Why don't you give her a call?"

It's perfectly permissible to be creative with these hooks. You don't have to have a commitment to travel to Tibet, or take up golf. You do have the passing thought, though, right?

By the way, you are apt to get the same response to your requests for introductions as you would to any direct-mail piece: 95 percent of people will forget you ever mentioned it, but 5 percent will show interest. If only 5 percent of your friends are out and about looking for dates on your behalf, that can only make your life more interesting.

But probably not interesting enough. Besides other people throwing a stranger into your social sphere, you'll need to ransack it yourself. Then, if your current connections fall short (as they most likely will), you will have to consider stretching yourself beyond your present boundaries.

Begin by taking a second look at your established network. Deliberately look around at your life—your office, your committees, your gym, your clubs—and notice who is available. Include women as well as men, because turning single benefits from available new girlfriends as well as potential dates.

You may need to get beyond some of your own biases first. Single or not, many of us look on other single adults with a critical squint—bruised fruit remaining after the best has been picked over. "I feel safer dating widowers," one woman stated. "They don't feel so . . . used." Another expressed her strong distaste for singles groups in her age range, explaining, "When I see packs of single people who are older, they look pathetic to me. I think of them as recycled people in a junky romantic flea market. I don't want to shop there."

That's certainly her right, but the fact is, sometimes you find a treasure in a flea market. What's more—let's face it, many of us, whether trash or treasure, are going to be single again. In our long lives, the majority of us cycle in and out of attachments due to death or divorce. If you are at the single part of that cycle, it doesn't make you a loser, any more than it changed you into a winner when you were at that attached part of the life cycle. But it does mean that you will want to pay close attention to those who are also at the single part of their life cycle. Timing, in other words, is a necessary substrate of new friendship and true love.

Many people report having found a new relationship within their social sphere once they scanned through different eyes. "We were on the same board"; "We biked for weeks in the same club"; and of course, the very common, "I've known him for years," "always found her attractive," "dated her thirty years ago and we found ourselves single at the same time."

Old friends and past lovers have a huge emotional appeal, in part because we project on them a feeling of authenticity that's hard to attach to a late-in-life stranger. You know how unsatisfying it is when an author introduces a whole new character three-quarters of the way through the book? It feels like an artificial device rather than something that really evolved in the character's life. But if that same author makes a minor character assume prominence later in the book, we have a sense of inevitability. "Aha," we think. "The seeds of that relationship were there all along."

If you think of your own life as a narrative, you might notice that you are similarly reluctant to add a fresh major character this late in the story. It's not necessarily a conscious resistance, and we are not all equally averse to plot change at this point. (Some of us are actually quite desperate for it.) But it is a hesitation that might impact your own dating choices or those of the men who meet you. At the very least it's something to be aware of and to be very very patient about. Time, and only time, will make the new and strange feel like family.

Even if you are eager for the new, you will still want to reexamine your social network with a lens wide enough to include your past, because old boyfriends, high school crushes, and college best friends have a way of cycling into single life at the same time you have. A wide lens will also extend the definition of *social network.* When you are married, the contractor who repairs your driveway is just another guy who doesn't show up when he says he will. Single, he might become flirtation practice.

Finally, you might consider taking steps to expand your own network in order to meet more people. There are two basic paths to the people you have yet to meet:

- Traditional venues.
- The virtual venue of the Internet.

Before you reject either or both out of hand, you might want to test the waters in the smartest ways possible.

Success at the most traditional venues has less to do with the virtues of any specific site (say, the auto mechanics course versus the art museum versus the bar at The Palm) than with how the social situation is structured. You will meet new people most easily by joining *ongoing groups with porous borders, where new people join in and you get to interact over time.*

For example, a class, however often it is recommended, is a less likely (not impossible, but less likely) place to connect with a man, because it's static. Classes meet for a limited period of time, with a fixed group of people who often have no easy way to set up an interaction outside of that class. That's why, as one woman reported, "I took tons of classes, checked for wedding rings, started conversations, and met a lot of nice women doing the same thing."

Fly business class to meet businessmen and you will rack up plenty of frequent flier miles, but successfully hooking up with the guy in the seat beside you requires being exceptionally attractive yourself, and/or exceptionally flirtatious. Even then, the chances of the taker's being married are exceptionally high. Be careful what you wish for.

But an ongoing group, like a shared beach house or ski house, offers more opportunity, because a core group gathers regularly, but friends of friends are welcome to come and go. Too old to tolerate a stranger's wet towel in the bathroom? No problem. Theater groups, political clubs, election workers, and/or any club where you play the sport, admire the art, enjoy the show, and then (here's the linchpin) *hang out afterward to discuss it* fits the description. In fact, many people skip the activity entirely and simply find a relaxed local bar in which to gather.

You don't have to drink to play. One woman discovered a brand-new over-forty community at 7 AM at Starbucks. "Of course," she said, "it made sense when I thought about it. People who don't have someone to have coffee with in the morning want that camaraderie. I met a whole interesting group of people who included me over time."

Over time is a key phrase here. You may have to show up somewhere—whether it's a bar or a bike club or a coffee shop—a dozen times before you feel comfortable. In the beginning it will seem like everyone knows everyone except you. That may or may not be true, but it will sure feel that way. Eventually, if you are there long enough, some extrovert will seek you out (assuming you aren't one yourself, because if you are, you won't have this problem) and voilà—you have new friends.

Meeting new people through traditional venues is easier if you have developed significant personal interests, because these interests form the common ground on which new relationships are founded. Maybe, though, in your heart of hearts, you are still so close to marriage and motherhood that you haven't figured out what your independent interests are. (That family was your interest, right?) Okay, don't be hard on yourself. A defined you will emerge from this lumpen identity confusion. Meanwhile, fake it with a little help from your past.

Think back to what you enjoyed when you were twelve or so. Did you play the guitar? Ice skate? Design doll clothes? Kick a soccer ball? Canoe? Sing a cappella? Read mysteries? Love puzzles? Test out some adult equivalent: the orchestra committee? Guitar lessons? Join a skating club? Take up chess? You get the idea. You might rediscover yourself there, as well as connect with other adults who have the same tentative thought.

Many women who rebuilt a social life solved the problem of their single isolation by relying on some club or activity as a lifeline.

"I joined the Mainline Ski Club and learned to ski at fifty. I loved it, and the ski club meant that I didn't need to have a date to have a good time. We could all go as a group. You have to reach out to that kind of thing—otherwise you will be spending all your time at home or just with women." Just with women is fine. If you want a romantic life, adding a few men is better.

All of this takes certain courage, of course. It requires a personal, internal push to get yourself outside your house, outside your comfort zone, and onto the ice. In the end, though, those risks turn out to be not such a big deal. One widow, determined to re-create a life, advised as follows: "If it's fun, great. If it's not, get in your car or call a cab and *go home*. It's not a big deal. The stakes are low."

Some would say the payoff is low too. Women who find sorting through the world at large for like-minded singles an overwhelming prospect might prefer to short-circuit the whole process. They go online, where those who are seeking meet fellow seekers. For better or for worse.

Online introductions have their fans and their detractors, and each side makes a fair point. On the plus side, there is just no likely alternative way that you could be exposed to so many single men in your area. A dating site offers women a sheltered situation in which to make the first approach, and some women find this unfamiliar power pleasant. Too, online dating is, for many, a safe form of fun, and a highly effective antidote to the initial loneliness of living alone. Sometimes computer dating is actually wireless hope.

Other times, it's tedious and exhausting. As one eHarmony burnout said, "The only thing you know about an Internet date is that this person has access to a computer." The sheer time-consuming chaff of faces, profiles, e-mails, and first dates you might sort through in search of that click of connection wears you down at least as often as it pumps you up.

E-mail fatigue is not the only downside of Internet dating. Online relationships create a pseudo-intimacy that can be deeply hurtful when it's lost. Ongoing correspondence gives us the illusion that we know someone, even that we *mean* something to each other. Then that someone vanishes into cyberspace for who knows what reason, or confesses to his actual age, gender, marital status, or waistline measurement. Much as you knew going in how much dishonesty exists on the Web, it still stings. It still feels like rejection; it still creates hopelessness—both at a time when you don't need one iota more emotional pain.

Be prepared for the reckless character of Internet encounters. Some people are lovely, yes. Some are ruthless liars. You will not be able to tell the difference online. It's a risk you take. Even relative truth tellers spin their stories, you can bet on it. And their pictures? To put it kindly, a picture is just a hint of what someone might resemble, or did resemble long ago. But so what? This is the Internet, and that's how it works.

You can protect yourself to some degree from these discouraging downsides of Internet dating. For one thing, when you first decide to go online, you'd be wise to do so with at least semi-professional guidance. There are better and worse ways to present yourself, and there's just no reason for you to discover all this by trial and error. At least scan a few of the books on Internet dating and write your profile according to the advice that best suits your individual interests.

Definitely ask a trusted friend to help you choose your photos. Absurdly, your photo makes a huge difference in your response rate—even though everyone knows that the person who shows up for coffee will only dimly resemble that picture. Still, an attractive photograph is key, and most of us are simply unable to see ourselves as others do. Since having others see you in a positive light is the point of this foray, an honest friend, particularly an honest male friend, could guide your choice best. You might as well have that same friend read over your profile at the same time, on the two-marketing-heads-are-better-than-just-nervous-you theory. It can't hurt.

Unless you're at the stage where you are just practicing e-mail flirtation, confine your correspondence to three or four e-mail volleys at most. Call your phone company, find out how to block your number, get his phone number, and move your interchange to the telephone. A telephone conversation connects you to the real world much faster, and you won't have so much emotionally invested in your e-mail fantasy lover.

A positive telephone call can be followed up by a brief escapable meeting, say for coffee or drinks, in (of course) a safe public place. This way you've vetted the person before he knows your name or number, and you don't have to go further unless you both like what you see.

These maneuvers should shield you from the potential hurt feelings of an Internet breakup. (Yes, you can get hurt even when you have never met the man. We're like that.) But they are no protection against the sense of discouragement that comes from sifting through the many to identify the sane. Online you will meet the normal and the paranormal. You'll have to pick your way slowly and carefully to tell the difference.

You can really only get the most out of Internet dating when you have the time and energy for it—which, come to think of it, is true of all dating, no matter how you meet potential partners. The Internet, though, does have some very distinct advantages that make it worthwhile.

Whether or not you meet someone with whom to form a relationship, the Internet is the very best place to learn to get comfortable with being single again. You'll practice flirting and rehearse answers to the questions men typically ask. You'll come to identify the men to whom you respond, and you might even get a glimpse of why. And, if you are like many women, you will become braver than you were when you started.

"I'm more flirtatious and open on a computer," one woman said. "It's an easy place to say whatever you want. If I'm intrigued by what someone has said about himself, I can send him a note. Actually, it's fun."

Your own reaction—whether to the traditional route, the virtual highway, or both—might depend on how new you are to being single, how much energy you have available to invest in flirting with strangers, and how much luck you have along the way. (Let's face it. Three bad dates in a row can send you limping back to the bench; two e-mails from promising strangers or a well-described fix-up from a friend can perk you right back up again.)

Eventually, though, if you keep at it, someone, somewhere will catch your fancy. Or you will catch his. And you will both proceed, inching forward, following E. M. Forster's famous directive: "Only connect."

Only Connect

You are at a bar with your friends and somehow, infrequent but still, a man at the far end of the bar appeals to you. How to meet him?

At last week's open house, you met an engaging architect and began to discuss the neighborhood. You'd like to continue the conversation.

There's an attractive, unknown person at your gym. You cross paths, but he has never acknowledged you in any way.

A friend has invited both you and a single man for dinner.

You found him sexy, but he never followed up. Is there any way you can?

It's just a cup of coffee with an Internet stranger, but from the moment you walked in, he appealed to you. What's your best foot forward?

Someone has finally registered on your radar. Maybe he's set off a tiny blip; maybe he's a major crush. You've waited some suitable period of time—anywhere from a matter of minutes in the bar to perhaps a matter of weeks in the gym—and he does not appear to be making that male move. Now what?

Certainly part of the answer to that question depends on your knowing what maneuvers might work. The rest depends on whether you are confident enough to make those moves, or whether you even believe you should. This brings us to a key element in the game: *Who does the picking?*

Who has generally done the picking in your romantic life story? Are you the woman who spots the guy and, one way or another, attracts his interest? Or are you the woman who waits to be picked? While this is not necessarily an either/or, if you think about it you might find you've been leaning one way or the other.

Regardless, you can learn to adjust in the other direction if you decide it would work better for you. The fact is, both strategies have their strengths and weaknesses. Best of all would be to have both in your repertoire.

Waiting to be picked is the traditional and often recommended female stance. It translates simply into waiting for a man to make the first move. He sends over the drink at the bar, he makes the first call, asks for the date, and, in general, risks the rejection.

Since being pursued rather than risking the rejection of pursuit is one of the few perks of being female in courtship, most of us are loath to give it up. Besides, there's all that stuff about the male of the species being a natural hunter and how huntresses turn them off and if he's interested, he'll call—so why bother considering anything else? These are all persuasive arguments for waiting to be picked.

If it's working for you, great. That is, if enough men who interest you are picking you with no inviting signal from you first, if they are crossing the room or making the call simply on the strength of your beauty and charisma, then you need go no further. (If that's the case, many people are offering you the opportunity and you are, in effect, doing the picking.)

But the rest of us, say the other 99.9 percent, are not always satisfied by waiting to be picked. We see attractive men but we don't quite know how to catch an eye. The men who do call may or may not be fine, but the ones who don't are sometimes interesting too. Or no one calls, and we're just plain tired of waiting to be picked. What then?

Then you will need to improve your skills at the ancient art of flirtation, because flirtation provides that necessary connective tissue: He still does the picking, but she signals in a very nice way that she'd be interested in being picked. What a great system. It does require a little practice, however, because we all lose the knack when we've been out of the game.

Flirtation is no more and no less than communicating to someone that you find him attractive. Flirtation is liking, warmth, and positive regard—with the kick of a sexual flicker. That's all. It's letting a man know—with a smile, an attentive gaze, with a compliment, a light touch, and a positive comment—that you find him an appealing person. As such, flirtation is a kind and charming way to interact with the world.

True, plenty of women and even more men make flirting a heavy-handed operation, with an obvious overemphasis on the sexual interest. While that may be stimulating to some recipients, it is discomfiting to many more. Hardly anyone wants to be put on the sexual spot unless there is a clear financial transaction involved. Even then, many men need alcohol to take advantage of the trade.

Delightful flirtation does not emphasize the sexual potential because it doesn't have to. Instead, there is the subtle suggestion of admiration and interest that an accomplished flirt sprinkles like M&M's through a crowd of good children. That said, when you are flirting with a single and noteworthy man, you are, in effect, sending a signal: "I find you attractive. Let's pursue this." That signal gets sent in a variety of ways, any of which might be right for you and for the situation.

The first way that signal gets sent is by placing yourself in physical proximity to him. In the scientific observation of flirting (naturally, there's a science of flirting), physical approach is step one of a five-step process by which two strangers make a connection. Timothy Perper, in his book *Sex Signals*, summarizes that research. Here, for the sake of furthering your scientific education, are those five steps:

- Approach.
- Turn.
- Talk.
- Touch.
- Synchrony.

These five steps happen in sequence, and if you and Mr. Handsome on the other side of the party waltz through all five, chances are something is definitely going on between you. To review them:

Approach. Approach is your first step in promoting the picking without actually intruding on male-role turf and making him nervous. Approach means that you put yourself in his physical proximity. If that's you with four girlfriends in a booth, you don't have to be so aggressive as to send a drink over to the guy at the end of the bar (though you could if you're in the mood), but you would want to leave the girlfriend pack and put yourself near where he is standing. If a man has noticed you and is drawn your way, he will do the same thing.

Turn. If you make an approach and he turns toward you, he is giving you an opening—whether consciously or unconsciously. If you turn toward a man who has put himself in proximity to you, you are offering a possibility of connection.

Talk. Then one or the other person will talk. If all is progressing, turning and talking will occur incrementally. That is, once you approach, if he turns toward you a bit, you'll say something. Probably something not very important, but something. He'll then turn toward you more, and you two will begin a conversation. Turn. Talk. Turn more. Talk more. It's all starting to happen.

It matters very little what is actually said. "Try the Merlot." "How's the bread?" "Do you live in the neighborhood?" work just fine. So does a more openhearted gesture, like the one this widow described:

"There was a man I knew casually whose wife died. I couldn't even convey my respects, because I didn't know him that well and it felt awkward. But one day about a year later, I saw him at the supermarket and I took a breath and went over to express my sympathy. I said, 'I know what it's like. I'm widowed too.' He called the next Monday and started asking me out. At first I wouldn't give him a chance, because I had decided he was too old. But one day, I remember exactly where I was, we danced together. Then and there I decided to give it a chance. Now he's part of my family." Approach. Turn. Talk. Touch. Synchrony. And then, the agony, ecstasy, and ambivalence of relationship.

Ahh, but we're not up to that yet. We are just getting back in the game, seeking players, so learning to risk the tiny boldness that might make a connection with an arousing stranger.

As stated earlier, most initial talk is just pleasantry for the purpose of furthering a connection. If one or the other of you stops talking and turns away, the sequence is over and you'd probably best move on to another prospect. This attractive man may have turned away from you for any number of reasons—he has a date, a girlfriend, or a wife; is too absorbed in the sport televised behind the bar to pay attention elsewhere; feels socially awkward; has a different agenda; something else is on his mind; or he just isn't interested. For whatever reason, you did not pass the lightning test with which we screen strangers. Or he didn't pass yours.

Touch. But should both of you wish to proceed, you will become absorbed in conversation. If the connection is strengthening, one or the other of you will probably reach out for some light touch. Remember, this is all automatic, instinctive, and probably barely conscious in everyone but the most deliberate of players. That light touch could be a quick hand pat, or an arm squeeze. In the days when everyone smoked, it was a brief handclasp as he held the lighter for her cigarette. Today it might be fingers brushing as you hand over a drink or offer an hors d'oeuvres plate. The light touch is certainly not intrusive or sexual. But it is a physical link, however brief.

Synchrony. Finally—sometimes in just fifteen minutes, and sometimes after two or three hours—two previous strangers now in a newly connected dyad will begin to make gestures in synchrony. Synchrony means that you two make the same movement at pretty much the same moment. It's not planned, it's not conscious, but it happens nonetheless. He crosses a leg as she crosses a leg, and in the same direction. Or she lifts her drink and he lifts his drink at the same instant. Again, synchrony isn't staged (unless you are really trying hard). It is simply what occurs as an association evolves.

So, if you want to flirt a bit with an appealing prospect—say, the guy to whom you haven't been introduced at the gym or the bar or the party—you might deliberately cross the room to be closer to him, turn to speak with him, and offer a friendly, inconsequential opening.

You have very little to lose, though every turn-away does smart for a few minutes. If your pang lasts longer than a few hours, or if the turn-away sends you home in tears, you are still way too vulnerable to play. You'd benefit from a lot more practice and more support. Frequent success is the ultimate balm for the sting of occasional rejection, but you can't experience that success without risk. If it's a fat, dumb, and ugly day and you are feeling especially shaky, then flirting with a stranger might not be the way to go.

Of course your attitude affects the outcome, although it's not exactly clear how that attitude is communicated. One recently separated woman talked about that exact phenomenon: "I was one of those married people who was just not looking around. When I was all of a sudden single and noticing who was out there, I could see that everything had to do with my state of mind—even though I don't know how it works. When I open up, things come in and men seem to appear. When I shut down, which I did when my dad got sick and when the divorce reached an ugly moment, well, nothing came my way."

When you know you are having a bad stretch, you might allow yourself some restorative hibernation. On the other hand, if you are having one of those invincible evenings, you can feel free to go to the other extreme. You can signal a total flirty come-on, for no better reason than it's fun to be the one coming on once in a while, just to see what happens. You might approach by, for example,

—sending over that drink,
—dropping your business card in his lap,
—mouthing the words *I love you* across the room,
—just walking straight up and saying, "I need to know who you are,"

or any other high-voltage connector that you might care to try.

Be forewarned, though: You may be flirting with the most innocent and playful of spirits; a man, however, is apt to at least consider the possibility that you are, in fact, a hooker who is seeking to attract his attention for commercial reasons. At the very least he is apt to see you as a desperate housewife. Just the daunting amount of conversation necessary to clarify these misconceptions might discourage you from taking the more direct and outrageous approaches to flirtation—however fun they might be once in a while.

Of course, there's a middle ground between "How's the Merlot?" and "I must tell you—I love your lips." That middle ground involves a strategy of bridge building.

Basically, once the conversation is under way, you are seeking an opening that will give this man grounds to call you. It won't make him call you if he's not interested. No great line can do that. But if he is interested, the opening you've suggested will make the phone call easier for him and therefore more likely. It's the follow-up flirtation signal that says, "If you want to continue doing this picking, I'm interested in being picked."

For example: "I ran into a man I've known at Home Depot. He stopped to talk to me, so that's what gave me the courage. We caught up for a few minutes and he mentioned he was moving. I asked if he was having a packing party, because I'd be happy to come. I'm sure he never even heard of a packing party, but he picked up on it and said, 'Well, if I do, how can I get in touch with you?' Bingo."

Or, as it comes up in your conversation: "I've been wanting to see that boxing match . . . check out that arboretum . . . try in-line skating, you make it sound so great . . . catch that IMAX show . . . try fly fishing . . . see that exhibit . . . learn more about the facilities at your club . . . visit that part of New Jersey . . . ." The point is to *give someone a reason to call you.*

You are also leaving yourself a reason to call him. Can a

woman/should a woman call a man? Well, she certainly can. And most men, just like most women, say that if the person calling is interesting and attractive, they are happy to get the call. If she's not, well, he feels just as awkward about that unwelcome call as you do. Still, calling a man to ask for a date feels to many women like they are uncomfortably close to an unflattering gender bender.

There are certainly women who will pick up the phone, call a man they met at a cocktail party, and simply state, "I wonder if you are free for dinner sometime." Sweet. Direct. Macho. Maybe too macho for you?

If it is, and it is for most of us, then you will feel more comfortable calling for a reason. That reason could

—have something to do with a subject that came up between you: "I'd love to see where those hiking trails are . . . find out more about the volunteer possibilities you mentioned . . . see those wood-burning stove outlets . . ."

—be a request for advice: "You mentioned your interest in wine and I'd love a recommendation for my next party" . . . "I'm car shopping and I wonder what you think of" . . . "What's your thought on contractors, real estate agents, marketing companies"—who cares what. Then, after you take the advice (or even if you don't), call him up and tell him you'd like to take him for a drink, to thank him for the free advice.

—be an invitation. Playing hostess gives you lots of opportunity to extend yourself to someone you don't know well: "I'm having people over to watch the game . . . for brunch on Sunday . . . for a cookout . . . and I'd love to continue our conversation." It doesn't really matter if he's free or not, because the invitation itself is an expression of interest. An invitation of the more traditional variety, as in "I happen to have two tickets to . . . ," is fine too. It all expresses the same intent—"I'm interested"—in a nice way.

Naturally, none of these ploys disguises your agenda, nor should they. You are expressing interest one tactful, gracious way or another, and he will either respond or not.

You can really only go a round or two before you come perilously close to being perceived as a stalker. But it does sometimes take a few back-and-forths before you can get on someone's radar. Lucy, for example, described pursuing a distant lover with uncharacteristic determination. "It was a year after my divorce and I think I was feeling complete helium. When I talked with the friend of a friend at a party, I knew I wanted a date with him. But he didn't call and there was no sign that he might. I figured, 'what the hell,' and I sent him an invitation to my annual Christmas party, which he promptly declined, saying he was traveling.

"I thought about it for a few days and then I actually called him, reminded him of who I was, and asked him to recommend the wine for the party. I think he was a little taken aback, but he made a suggestion. The wine turned out to be pretty good, so nothing lost there. After Christmas, I left him a message telling him that I wanted to leave him a bottle of wine to say thanks. That was an easy gesture because I'd thank anyone who extended himself on my behalf. He called back to say, 'How about we meet for a drink, and you can give me the wine then?' Yay! He turned out to be worth the work too."

Lucy swears she would have quit at the thank-you wine if he still hadn't responded. You too will have to learn when to take no for an answer. Remember, though, that with flirtation, it is sometimes worth risking several nos. After all, men in pursuit do that all the time.

Well, maybe they do, but let's face it—you're not used to it. You've been out of the game too long to have developed the toughness to slough off rejection and the lighthearted spirit that makes flirtation more about fun and less about judgment. It's those first steps that can be difficult—those icebreakers. Whether the ice you are breaking is around your own heart, or it's the ice between you and the social world—the end result will be the same: You'll get comfortable getting naked again and develop your own best game. It starts, remember, in your head.

Attitude Check

Was this supposed to be fun? Well, certainly fun at moments, high at moments. But there are many anxious moments too, and you won't be the first woman who popped a Xanax prior to a first date, or poured a glass of wine and pretended it was to be social when actually it was to self-medicate. Truthfully, a little of this nerve management is not a bad thing. Not something to be entirely proud of, certainly, but not a sign of major mental illness either. A little pharmaceutical courage to push you past a scary moment is probably preferable to a life lived on the sidelines, where there is no anxiety to reduce because there is no risk you are willing to confront.

If you are hitting the wine every night, if you find you can't sleep without it, if you are relying on anti-anxiety meds to make it through most social encounters, well, we both know you have a different level of problem. But the point is that most of us have to get through a small rush of anxious arousal when we walk into that coffee shop to meet Mr. Match, or answer the door for Mr. Blind Date, or take the awkward walk together at the end of the evening and manage the kiss/don't kiss moment. Yes, I recognize that we are all long past nineteen and nervous. But these are inherently awkward human moments, and fifty gets frightened too.

All drugs and deep breathing aside, the single best way to put more fun and less fret into these experiences is to lower your expectations and cut yourself and the guy across the table a break. The change of expectation that reduces your anxiety is all about the attitude you bring to the game.

In chapter 4 we discussed your attitude at length, and I recommended a philosophical shift to the here and now. After all, when the long-term stakes are lower, so is your stress level. (That's why you can be flirtier in France than in Cleveland.) I'm just reminding you here, as we discuss dating itself, that your frame of mind and your sense of purpose make all the difference in your success.

So, to review: Slow down and resist your urge to hunt for The One. Shift your thinking, if only temporarily. At this moment you are not looking to immediately pair off with that special person. You are looking, for a little while, to date the many.

You are just trying to buy yourself some time; to give yourself an opportunity to feel more like yourself, even though this is a self who never expected to be on a date again. This temporarily open attitude, however useful, will not be easy to develop. Frankly, spend any time in the game and you too will end up looking for The One pretty quickly.

Given the medical, sexual, and social pressures of monogamy, our emotional need for security, and the limited pool of people with whom we can make an authentic connection, most of us tend to move from dating to relationship in a nanosecond or less. We are quickly funneled from the many to the one, and then we make every attempt to turn that one into The One.

This sorting, seeking, and selecting process is nearly inescapable. The only men and women who avoid it are those who prefer—usually for reasons of past injury, intense self-involvement, or both—to live life at an emotional distance from others. The far distant may have long histories of dating the many, attaching to the few, and, even then, not attaching very deeply or very generously.

But these are men and women who are at a particular emotional extreme. In the middle, most of us date until we connect and then abandon dating with relief, concentrating on the precarious process of constructing a satisfying relationship. We'll talk about the common problems and patterns of those early relationships in chapter 8.

First, though, like it or loathe it, give yourself some opportunity to date. *Dating* here is used loosely, to include anything from a first meeting in the park ("I'll be the one carrying *Tropic of Cancer*," he said. "Never mind," she said.) to an encounter

with a premature ejaculator who showers after. Your own experience of dating may involve formal phone calls, invitations,
pick-you-ups and walk-you-to-the-doors; or you might be expected to participate in the show up at the same party, hang out
for a while, buy you a drink, and let's have sex version of dating
currently favored by the under-thirty single set. Or both. Or
something in between.

However briefly you allow yourself to linger in the dating
window, though, an in-the-moment attitude will maximize
your dating experience. A date, even a lousy can't-see-myself-
with-him-ever date, can pay off in several ways:

- It can make you feel attractive because, pure and simple,
  if someone who has met you is taking you to dinner, he
  is doing it because he finds you appealing. This can be
  balm to a woman recovering from loss—if you allow it,
  that is, if you aren't busy disqualifying the source, because, for one reason or another, he is unlikely to be The
  One.
- You might learn about some new field of endeavor from
  a man who is its expert, because men are apt to be very
  forthcoming about their work or their avocations if you
  appear interested. If you can leave an evening knowing
  something that you didn't know when you started—
  whether that knowledge is as practical as the proper way
  to assemble mulch or as arcane as historic train stations
  that have since been demolished—the evening's take-
  away has value.
- You can practice flirting, because it takes time for most
  of us to find our flirt when we begin to get naked again.

Dating whomever is a form of target practice. You get better at hitting the bull's-eye.

- You may discover a surprising restaurant, see a film, hear music you might not otherwise have chosen, be introduced to a different social circle. Quite often in early dating, men choose the activities. While the downside is that you can spend time in some truly tedious activities (golf, for example, would qualify for some of us) for the simple pleasure of his company, the upside is that you are sometimes introduced to a world of pleasure from a simple date (golf, for example, to the rest of us).

- You might get some free advice, because many men will offer themselves as experts in some area where you are having a legal, business, financial, marketing, or negotiating problem. Sometimes they actually are experts and the advice is priceless (plus, it's free). Sometimes, of course, they are not, but you will probably know the difference.

You can get any or all of these pluses out of an evening with the wrong date, the dull date, the date who talks with his mouth full. No, it doesn't add up to anything, it's not apt to go anywhere, it's not life altering. But here-and-now experience can have an impact too, if you are open to it. An appreciation of that impact makes you more open to meeting and dating the many, from whom it's possible that you will make a wiser choice of The One.

Along the way you will become sensitive to the fact that you are not learning to connect in a vacuum. You are a part of a social world that looks with interest on your efforts and your successes. And occasionally, let's face it, someone in your social world steps back in suspicion. After all, sometimes one woman's connection is another woman's husband.

CHAPTER SIX

Other Women and Their Husbands

I recently attended a very grown-up dinner party—grown-up as in art objects scattered on the table, wine the price of my first car, and plenty of ginger in the food. We were two married couples and two dating couples, known only to the hostess before this dinner. "Oh goody, new friends," is what I arrived thinking.

Normally I prefer to sit next to my date, so I can play footsie under the table if I am bored, but the host and hostess were long married and possibly past footsie, so they seated guests apart from their partners. I sat where I was assigned and watched the action.

The only other single woman was seated next to my date and immediately began to operate on him. She threw a body block to the rest of the table, engaged him in intense and remarkably admiring conversation, complete with gentle arm strokes. I observe them clink glasses. I hear her ask sweetly, "Does your wife enjoy that too?"—tactfully fishing for his availability. "Oh, that's not my wife," he quickly clarifies. She sighs. He knocks over his wine.

Eventually, tired of feeling like dog meat at my end of the table, I contrive a few minutes alone with my date. We make out and, while I suspect that it was her arm strokes that got his motor going, I decide not to care. When I return to the table she has turned her attentions to the married man on her right. This time she is facing me and I am treated to their dialogue. He: "You are a very passionate woman." She: "You are an unusually sensitive man." A few tears (I AM NOT KIDDING) run down her cheeks. He wipes them away with a napkin.

I look around the table, but no one appears to be noticing. His wife is across the table discussing spoiled teenagers. The single wolverine's date appears calm and pleasant. Am I the only person with sexual sig-naling on the brain? Is everybody else at this table really concentrated on whether the Merlot bouquet enhances the veal?

Meanwhile, the husband and the wolverine are exchanging e-mail addresses so they can continue their sensitive and passionate discovery of each other later. For one wild minute I imagine that I am at a 1950s key party where everyone swaps wives. But no, I don't think it's that. I think it's that the other women at the table are married and so long insulated in the armor of relationship that the sexual signals are not being received. Just in case, though, shortly after dessert my date and I leave. Together. I kiss everyone good-bye but the wolverine. She only nods to me. We are on to each other.

Sexual dynamics are not attending simply this party, of course, but many parties, as well as office assemblies, bar stool congregations, committee meetings, and gallery openings.

That dynamic is the boy-meets-girl, wonder-who's-cute, let's-make-a-connection unspoken agenda of people on the prowl.

For sure not every single woman or man is on the prowl. Maybe not even most. But plenty are, in one style or another, because that is the natural way in which people meet and mate. Also for sure, not every married person resists that natural impulse to prowl, whether he should or not. But you knew that already.

You may or may not have been tuned in to this covert sexual drama during your sheltered relationship years. Many women report that they were utterly oblivious and that the flirtations or affairs of friends always came as a complete surprise. Others—perhaps more experienced in the ways of attraction, flirtation, or betrayal—maintain interpersonal radar whatever their current relationship status. Whichever level of awareness describes you best during the years when you were safely attached, one thing is certain—the below-the-surface sexual dynamic is apt to hit you in the face when you are single. And you will need to know how to handle it.

It's tricky. Some men who are not unavailable (worse, some of whom are married to your friends) will try to find out if you are. Some available men will see you as desperate, when you only invited them for dinner. Some married women will resent you as a sexual threat, whether you are or not. And some single women will consider you roadkill on their way to impress a man.

No, this is not enough reason to climb back under the covers—except occasionally. You will learn, over time,

—to firmly signal *no* to the married hopefuls without losing their friendship;

—to extend invitations to single men with a light touch and a sense of humor;

—to step tenderly around the feelings of every married friend, because her anxiety level around you is your problem;

—to cherish the single girlfriends who are your true buddies and recognize the wolverines who may come disguised as gentle lambs. In the end, this one is easy. Your gut will know the difference. Trust it.

You will refine your interpersonal skills in each of these areas as you come to appreciate the powerful impact your change of relationship status has had. As you turn single, you don't do it alone. Your social world turns with you. Or against you.

Other Women

The divorce, the death, the desertion happened to you. And then it happened to the rest of us, to each person connected to you. However wide the circle, your loss ripples through it. It evokes our compassion; it threatens our security. It makes us clutch tighter to our own still-present partners, or think again about letting go. We grieve with you, or rage alongside you, even if it is only a pale echo of your own grief or anger. We feel all this for you and we feel it for ourselves. And it changes things.

Turning single is an inner evolution, as we've just discussed, and it's probably a hair and wardrobe makeover too. Beyond that, like it or not, turning single may impact your friendships in unexpected and painful ways. It will take the edge off your hurt feelings if you understand what's going on.

It's important to note that not every newly single woman will experience painful friendship changes, and that some friendship changes that occur will be quite positive. Widows speak from the heart about the depth of friendship they were offered. For many, friendship created a bridge of support over the dark river of loneliness and loss that would have engulfed them otherwise. Many mentioned with deep appreciation the compassion of friends who appeared to shovel snow, sort through insurance papers, decipher medical bills—offering life-sustaining practical and emotional aid through long months of incapacitating mourning.

True friendship is not solely the purview of widows. Lucky and loved divorced women also receive the support and compassion of giving friends:

> I had a girlfriend who called me every single Friday night to invite me to join her and her husband at our club for dinner. She knew I wouldn't want to sit there alone. I think of her as my guardian angel.

> Close friends, who knew I was overwhelmed, just got in their car, filled it with empty boxes, drove two hours to my house, and cleaned out my garage. That lighter load in the garage somehow made me turn an emotional corner. What a gift.

Divorcées and widows who signal a readiness to reenter the social world sometimes report blessed friends who do the spadework for them:

> About a year after my husband died, my friends at work decided I was ready, so they took up a collection and bought

me an introductory year with a professional matchmaker. Everyone reviewed my dates, and that's how I met the man I'm living with.

A friend who knows everyone in town took out her Rolodex and called every person listed who was single. She figured single people would know other singles, and she was right. She told every one of them that I needed to meet people and asked them to fix me up. Wow. Is there a friendship sainthood?

My close circle of friends continues to include me in everything. My ex-husband dropped away from them, which was a break for me because there hasn't been a conflict yet. We go out as we always did—to the movies, to dinner, whatever. Only now we are seven, instead of eight. I appreciate their loyalty so much, but I also know that I'm hiding out there. If I want to meet any new people, I'm going to have to do something else on Friday or Saturday nights. I don't want to, but I have to.

Therein lies the built-in problem, even for those women fortunate enough to have inclusive friends and guardian angels. Dating requires a different kind of reaching out into the social world. Single people meet each other, flirt with each other, date each other, sleep with each other, and just generally connect with each other in some separate, parallel universe. You may have been oblivious to this universe during the years when you were otherwise preoccupied with marriage or the kids or work. But if you are considering a reentry into romantic life, you will want to edge into this other world. And you'll want some single friends to keep you company.

So even if your lifelong friends and acquaintances are loving and supportive angels who are apparently unaffected by your giant life change, you will still have to reach beyond them to make new connections. You'll still need a couple of great single girlfriends, because your married friends will give stale advice (they just don't remember how it is, they've been married too long) or they won't be free to come out and play. (While they love you and they'd enjoy it, they're *married*. They are not free to practice flirting at the gym, and practice is what you need.)

Unless you have a ready stock of single girlfriends (and you may—divorces and even deaths tend to come in clusters in social groups, and you can help one another), you will need to make some. Making new friends—like forming any new important relationship—takes an investment of time, a certain amount of luck, a concentrated effort, and the risk of rejection. Put all that in and a year or so from now you will be close to and enjoying people who might not even be on your Christmas card list today.

You'll need those new friendships even more if your old friends turn out to be not so great. For an awful lot of us, that's the case. It hurts, sometimes as much as the divorce itself. Sometimes more.

For many women, turning single means losing their place in the social circle. You really do become the cheese standing alone—whether in their eyes, in your own, or in some blurred combination of both. Some social circles simply turn on the concept of couple and have no room to fit a single woman. Why?

Well, you might speculate that on some level you are a threat, and you'd be right. (We'll get to that in the next section.) You might assume that some people are avoiding financial awkwardness—when the men are divvying up the check, how should they handle you? Easier if you're just not there. Or you might conclude that these were never deeply rooted friends in the first place, just married people engaging in the social ritual of passing Saturday night. You no longer qualify for the club. The experience of being left out is common, and any or all of these explanations might apply.

My married friends dropped me from their radar after my husband died. If they are going out with mutual friends, they don't think to call me. But I don't find that hurtful. It's just how things are.

People don't fix me up, and I don't see my close married friends anymore. You become that extra woman that no other woman needs around.

My girlfriend asked me to babysit for her granddaughter on a Saturday night when she and her husband and another couple went to dinner. When I told her that it hurt my feelings to be excluded from the dinner, she said "Really? I just didn't think you'd want to come." But she never invited me in the future either.

Sometimes, maybe more often than you think, it's you who has moved beyond the married circle. What worked before is less satisfying or less comfortable now that you are single.

"I'm pretty and I'm confident. My old friends invite me out but I never go. I don't like being a third wheel."

"I go to the movies alone a little, but in the movies we used to hold hands and now it's like a phantom limb. I keep looking for that hand to hold. I don't want to be sitting next to another couple when they are holding hands."

"I don't want to be the one single one in a group of couples. It's like wearing a dunce cap."

"This is horrible, but I don't go out with my married friends anymore because my friends' husbands are so boring. I find them dull—they go on and on and on. Now that I'm single, I can enjoy my girlfriends at lunch and leave them to suffer through their husbands' prostate stories."

One way or another, husbands are part of why your relationships with your married girlfriends may have changed. Husbands—those men in the background whose friendships you may have enjoyed, or whose long anecdotes you may have tolerated for the sake of your girlfriend or your own partner—have now transformed into some other form of beast or beauty. They are, quite suddenly, *men*.

Other Women's Husbands

Janice, married for thirty years and divorced for two, spoke for many of us when she explained, "How do I know if I'm attractive to men? Or even what man I might like? You know, I was faithful. I was loyal. I hated my husband's guts, but I was not looking around. I was *married*."

Now suddenly you're looking. The first people in your line of sight will be your friends' husbands. And they will be looking at you.

When her husband fell in love with someone else and had some kind of guilty nervous breakdown, Hollie still had twin daughters at home, finishing their senior year in high school.

With her ex-husband alternately disappearing for weeks into his new fun life and returning to heap large gifts on his daughters and ignore her completely, Hollie hung on to whatever pieces of her old life she could preserve.

One ritual she treasured was an annual weeklong camping trip, traditionally shared by five families of friends who'd begun camping together when they'd met at their kids' preschool so many happier years earlier. The adults had remained close, the kids had gone on to form separate lives, but everyone enjoyed the one-week reunion. This year, Hollie determined, would be no different.

But it was. Hollie felt the awkwardness of being a single woman at the first planning breakfast. "I've always been the organizer, and my friends were still looking to me to do that. But I've always done that organizing with one of the husbands, because we are the two control freaks in the group. It was all fun, all laughing, but when I felt him looking across the table at me and mentioning that he'd call me so we could nail down the details, well, I felt a new energy between us. It just didn't feel comfortable and I didn't know how to handle it. Am I being oversensitive?"

I don't think so. I think Hollie is sensing a certain invisible shifting of the emotional plates around her. The new alignments may fall back precisely where they always rested, or some connections may move in very different directions. What Hollie is feeling—what you might sense too, whether temporary or permanent—is that shift.

Remember when Eddie Fisher comforted Elizabeth Taylor after Mike Todd died? Eddie was a good friend indeed, Liz was certainly a friend in need, and pretty soon Debbie Reynolds was divorced and checking out other people's husbands on her own behalf. Theirs is the cautionary tale that stirs in the back of many a wife's mind when a dear friend is suddenly single and she asks your husband for help with the storm windows. On the one hand, we understand that good friends deserve help; on the other, there is a tickle of concern that they might help themselves to our husbands.

Are divorcées and widows suddenly transformed by loneliness or freedom into sexual predators? No. Not at all. Period. Most newly single women report no interest, no poaching, no flirting, no boundary crossing of any variety. *But*—

Just as Hollie unexpectedly experienced, a neighbor smiling at you across the table does feel different to you without your husband sitting by your side. And if that husband has been smiling at some other woman lately, you could be especially needy and in search of male affirmation.

Turning single, you could feel something different for the friend who kindly hoists your air conditioner into place, even though he did it last year too, when your husband had the flu. This year he's doing it for you. Paying attention to you. Feeling something for you. And it will feel—*different*.

Different might be anxious, or awkward, or sexy, or high. Your feelings might broadcast loudly or be only faintest whisper. But you notice your emotional attention has shifted. Where once, as in Hollie's case, you may have been preoccupied with the question of your husband's other woman, now you find yourself reacting to other women's husbands.

Your attention shifts naturally, because becoming single makes many women study the men and relationships around them in a whole different way. After all, even if your friends' husbands are in your line of sight, it doesn't necessarily mean you will like what you see. It does usually mean, though, that you will be trying to figure it out.

"I do look at my friends' husbands differently," Caitlin explained, "but it's not in any way to flirt with them. I look at them and I ask myself, 'If this man were single, would I be attracted to him?' It's more a matter of trying to figure out what I like. Honestly, I hardly ever see a husband I'd like if he were free. What does that mean?"

It's a common sentiment. High-powered Joan, who spoke earlier about her tendency to disappear into her professional identity, did acknowledge that these days she makes an automatic sexual and romantic assessment of the crowd. "Sure," she said, "I certainly walk into a room now and ask myself, 'Is there any man here I could be boinking?' Or 'Who here has a sick wife?' But frankly, it's rare that anyone in my age group looks good to me."

It's normal for you to be looking around. You are looking to discover something about yourself, and about what opportunities might be available. You may find yourself studying relationships more closely than you did before—paying attention to who holds hands, who criticizes, who compliments, who dominates. You may start noticing

—how few good relationships there seem to be and how relieved you are to go home alone.
—what was good about your last relationship that perhaps you failed to appreciate at the time—or what was unspeakable that you can't believe you endured.

—how some women are bitchy and whiny and get far nicer men than they seem to deserve.

—how some women are doormats and mice and will put up with anything and you wonder why.

Through all these very private observations, you may mentally try on relationships with these husbands, just to identify your own reaction. "Not him," you might think. "Uck. Could never kiss him. And not him either, he's waaay too fat. But maybe, maybe, one like him."

So long as these fantasies are cause for self-discovery, so long as you never, never, never take a step in that husband's direction, you are on safe ground. Just feeling for a moment that there is some man on the planet who might appeal to you is an energizing vision. Okay, not this man of course, because he is not available. But if there's one, there are others, and your thoughts have, in effect, primed your pump.

Still, what if, inadvertently, unconsciously, or, worse, deliberately, you do take a step toward him? Or he thinks you have, or, worse, your girlfriend thinks you have? In other words, you are living a twist on the classic question, which in your case has become "Can a married man and a single woman ever be friends?"

No matter what your personal opinion on the age-old question of male and female friendship, you can maintain stability in your own social circle if you keep one rarely discussed friendship dynamic front and center in your thinking: All friendship is something of a magnetic attraction between two people. And sexual appeal is a part of that magnet.

Something—some spark, some spirit, some attractive energy—

draws you together. Then social, psychological, and situational pressures quickly squish the sexual energy deep into a safe, unconscious place. Think Al Gore's "lockbox" if you want an idea of how far below the surface sexuality can be stashed.

If the sexual piece is there, it's there as the merest whisper. Consider your girlfriend's husband, say, or your married office buddy. He's your friend. He gives you stock tips or parenting advice because he likes you and gets along with you. He's not hitting on you, not thinking of you sexually except in the way that men automatically decide about all women ("Would I fuck her or not?"). But he's not singling you out for a starring role in his erotica. You are his office friend or his buddy's wife and he's got a wife of his own.

The sexual thread is buried, thrust automatically into that psychic lockbox. Neither of you feels it. Neither of you is uncomfortable. And then you turn single and the lid blows off the box.

You are available. You are needy. Or he thinks you might be, which is erotic enough for him. The sexual urge, safely tucked away, sneaks into the air between you. Or this married man's sexual urge may never have been tucked safely away at all. Or his wife, sensitized because perhaps his urges have leaked out on other occasions, is imagining his reaction to you. Or watching it.

As a woman turned newly single, you may not even realize any of this. One widow related her single education. "At a dinner party, a man gave me his business card and suggested I call him about something and we could discuss it over lunch. My girlfriend saw it and said to me later, 'You've been married way too long.' She thought he was hitting on me and I missed the signals because his wife was sitting right next to him. Now I try to be a little more alert to what's going on around me."

Whether these are the husbands of your friends, your acquaintances, or just some random husband who crosses your path, you will need to be prepared for the interest of the married man and for the sensitivity of that married man's wife. Both require tactful management.

The same widow who was so naive at the dinner party quickly received a social education. "I've belonged to a wonderful club for many years without a single knee pat in my direction. But about six months after my husband died, two or three husbands tried their luck with me. In the beginning I thought they were being friendly and supportive—you know, inviting me to a club lecture or a wine tasting, I thought, because we shared those interests. But every time, somewhere in the course of the evening, the subject of sex came up. Somewhere. Somehow. And believe me, not by me.

"The funny thing was, more than one of these guys happened to mention his lesbian fantasies—just, you know, as a topic of general conversation. Do you think it's my short hair?" She laughed, but kept moving.

Most of us laugh and keep moving, although you know and I know that some single women pause to sample the wares. Mostly, though, single women report moving on in a clear, firm fashion once they realize what's happening.

"One friend's husband did come on to me," said a recently widowed professor. "His wife is always away in the summer and my husband and I always invited him to dinner. I just naturally continued the tradition and invited him over the summer after my husband died. Over wine he said, 'Oh, if I weren't married, I could really go for you.' I said, 'Well, you are, so you don't have to think about it.' I still see him, but I always make sure that it's when his wife can come to dinner too."

Part of developing your interpersonal expertise is becoming sensitive to situations that may not have been issues when you were attached. Your married girlfriend's sense of security is one of those issues. It's not fair that you have to be concerned when in fact you have no interest in your girlfriend's lumpish mate, but hey—what's fair? If you are newly single, and you want a happy girlfriend, you want to avoid even the appearance of a sexual buzz with her spouse.

It's not that tough to do if you maintain awareness. Just avoid any private lunches, dinners, or evenings with your friend's husband. Yes, he's your broker and you've always met for business meals. Meet in his office instead. You're single now, and that changes the dynamics of everything.

If you have a private phone call with a friend's spouse, make sure you mention it to her later. Be a bit careful about how you hug him or kiss him. Put an inch between your bodies. It's an inch that announces a clear boundary. If he comes over to help you, make sure your girlfriend knows that she's welcome to come over too.

You may find all this wildly unnecessary, because you believe that in your long-standing friendship circle, sexual attraction is the very last thing on anyone's mind. And maybe you're right. Or you might resent the idea that you have to make special efforts to reassure girlfriends who ought to know you better by now. Okay. They should. Besides, you're the one whose life is in an upheaval. How come you have to take care of their feelings when they should be looking out for you? All true.

But bending over backward costs very little and works well. It's a just-in-case strategy that has a hidden benefit to you. If you manage the relationships with social savvy, the interest of other women's husbands can revive you. They are, after all, men.

It will remind you that the interest of men, the support of men, the sexual energy of men, the companionship of men, their size and money and jokes and smell and physical knack and stash of useful technical lore—are all things you'd like to add back into your life. That's your motivation for dating.

And that's why even you might risk getting naked through one of dating's three great venues for self-exposure or cover-up: Conversation, Sex, and Money.

CHAPTER SEVEN

Conversation, Sex, and Money

She waits in the car, grabbing for her cell phone the instant her son disappears into the gas station convenience store to pick up a coffee. This is not a conversation for sons, even thirty-year-old ones. She calls a girlfriend and skips right through the hello to

"I don't know what to wear."

"Who cares what you wear if you're taking your clothes off?" her girlfriend points out, remembering that this is the day of her friend's first sexual encounter since the divorce.

"I know. But we're spending the night and he mentioned something about taking a hike together. I don't know if he meant before or after, but I just can't see myself turned on to sex while unlacing my hiking boots, you know?"

"Yeah, well, maybe sex first to break the ice, then the hike, then you could actually enjoy sex again later when you're more yourself?"

"Jane—he's sixty-one years old. I'm thinking sex twice in a day could be a little ambitious."

"Okay, so how about you let him run this show and you just

go with his program? You aren't married anymore, sweetie. That means you don't have to do all the work by yourself."

"We can only hope," she said, but she liked the idea. This man gave every appearance of being able to carry out a plan with competence. That was why she had decided she wanted to sleep with him in the first place. "I think his hands look very capable," she said.

"Shut up." Her girlfriend laughed. "I'm getting so turned on I might have to fuck my husband."

The son appeared at the passenger door of the car carrying his cup of coffee. "Gotta go," she said into the cell phone. "Thanks. Love you." She hung up the phone and returned to the demeanor of motherhood. Hiking boots were coming off later.

*F*irsts. In the process of getting naked again, firsts are very big. First e-mail, first phone conversation, first face time, first kiss, really, with someone other than your husband. First sexual experience with a new lover should you decide to go that far, first bringing someone back to your home, your bed, first meeting the kids. Every step, even the ones you decide to skip, is part of the process.

Any or all of these first-time events might occur in jumbled-up order. Some potential partners meet the family and never make it to the bedroom. Other women prefer sexual hookups who live out of town and never intrude on their living space or real life. Whichever steps come easily, a few will probably make you hesitate. So much of what you are experiencing is difficult to fit into your picture of yourself or of your partner.

One abruptly abandoned mother of three described how many of her "firsts" occurred mostly in her own mind. "The big thing for me," she said, "was to put another man in my head besides my husband. I was very conditioned to being with one person. Good or bad, I was aware of how we operated as a couple. '*This* is how my ex was,' I'd think—even in something small like how we were in a restaurant, whether he was friendly or not, or bossy or not, how we would navigate a menu.

"It's all different on a date, because now there is a different man on the other side of the table. For a long time I was saying to myself, 'Oh, this is different. Is this good? Do I like this? Hey, this is better than I had it before.' It takes awhile to get used to it. Every experience you did as a couple, you are replaying with a new personality and trying it on for size. For a long time my constant comparing kept me on the outside looking in. It kept me in a critical, evaluative place that was safer for me, I guess. It took me a long time to relax whatever vigilance that was and be more a part of the dates I was having."

Even if you have been dating for some time, you might reexperience that sense of first again—say, with a new partner, or at a different stage in the lives of your children, or in a different location. Dating is discomfort, until it gets comfortable. And even then, let's face it, it can get a little weird.

What's great about getting naked at this point in your life is that you can set a pace to suit yourself and make up the rules as you go along. You will probably need to adjust those rules from time to time, because what works best for you may not be immediately obvious. You'll need to allow yourself some romantic experimentation, and that requires risk.

Depending on your nature and comfort level, you might be

a woman who prefers her risks in bite-size pieces, or you might be someone who launches herself into an affair and looks up six months later to see what part of herself is left standing. Both work, and each has its cost. (But you knew that. You're a grown-up now and you know there's no free lunch.)

Bonnie described her own experience of getting naked again as a tiptoe. "My goal for this year was to have sex at least, and maybe, maybe, to have a relationship. Believe me, I was a long way from sex, so I went online because that was a private way to put myself out there. I picked some metro Web site and I don't know why. Maybe because they asked for less information.

"I got a huge range of responses and I was terrified. First I only wanted to do an e-mail thing, and I did that for a while. Most of those connections faded very quickly, just a few e-mails and then it all stopped.

"Then I met a couple of guys for coffee and maybe once for a drink. The meetings lasted, oh, I'd say under an hour. Nothing went further than that first meeting for months. Sometimes they followed up, sometimes not. But I said no to anything more.

"The whole experience at this point was really all about me—it was about gathering material directed by some internal monologue like, 'What will I notice about someone? What will I find attractive?' Online was a comfortable, manageable way to learn what I was okay with or not. Frankly, I got more of a sense of what I don't like—men my own age, men with beards—than what I do like.

"Plus, I had some conversation with myself that went, 'Meet a man? What's that like? Kiss a man? What's that like?' Every time I took a tiny step, I could think, 'Well, I did that. That's not so scary.'"

Tiptoeing is not everyone's preferred pace. Greta flung her whole heart into a love affair with a bachelor she met eleven months after her own astonishingly speedy divorce was negotiated. The new man was a stranger, but not entirely unknown to her—an available man whom a friend introduced, suggesting she might find him interesting. (Months later that same friend defended herself vigorously. She'd never meant for Greta to fall in love with this fellow so perfectly unsuited for love. She'd been thinking dinner, or at most a brief sexual spin. Just something to get Greta's feet wet after a long marital dry spell.)

But Greta did fall in love, complete with the heart squeeze, the thrill, the insane longings and ecstatic reunions that accompany such experiences. A year and many tears later, Greta had progressed from being wildly in love to settling down to a limited but not entirely unfulfilling relationship. It took still another year for Greta to let go of Mr. Limited and face turning single alone. In the end, when Greta assessed the damages, she felt she'd come out ahead. "That experience showed me I could feel something again. That life isn't over."

In fact, at whatever pace you choose to enter the game, you too will find that romantic life is not over. At every new encounter it begins again—with a conversation.

Come Here Often?

In a way, a relationship is one long conversation—even in the hard times when you've stopped speaking. Lost partners are conversations interrupted, though they may continue with life-like accuracy in your mind. Widows ask absent spouses, *"What should I do?"* and sometimes hear a clear suggestion; divorcées continue to defend themselves against an imagined critical remark, though the old critic doesn't live here anymore. Conversation dies hard.

For some of us, it starts hard too. A romantic relationship may begin with that indefinable instant of visual attraction and emotional appeal that we call chemistry. Quickly, though, sometimes simultaneously, a connection is established through conversation. The pressure is on, which is why "What the hell am I going to talk about?" is an initial obstacle faced by so many newly returned to dating. When you come across a serial dater who has a formulaic approach, you find it hard to feel you've met the man behind the interview.

You certainly can't program early dating conversation to create a connection with everyone, any more than you can reshape your face, your body, or your aroma to have universal appeal. (Ahh, but wouldn't that be a fun way to live.) But you can take two strategic steps to get out of your own way:

- You can exercise some discipline in how you present yourself.
- You can learn to risk more open-ended unfolding, and so connect more easily and more authentically.

Neither of these is difficult, but both require some degree of conscious effort, because they may go against your immediate impulse.

Conversation on early dates is aimed at achieving several ends: establishing common ground, presenting your romantic credentials, and assessing his. A positive emotional connection is established through some pleasant balance of each, but that's not always an easy equilibrium to achieve.

On the one hand, you want to lay back and serendipitously discover that you both admire Werner Herzog's films and you concur that the Eagles' quarterback needs replacing. At the same time, if you are seeking a relationship (remember, not everyone is), you are each probably listening hard for some red light/green light of your own devising—is he rude, dull, scornful of women? Is she whiny, demanding, or just generally unhappy? It's a lot of work for a cup of coffee, but hey—that's dating.

Part of the emotional effort of dating is figuring out, *bit by bit*, who this person is, as you reveal yourself, *bit by bit*, to him. Think of this presentation of self as a social résumé, which includes:

- The relationship basics: Married how long? Separated still? Divorced or widowed, how long? Dating someone now or totally available? Plus, of course, the story of how it all unfolded.
- Family basics: Children, grandchildren, and the all-important, do they live with you and/or do they speak to you? Plus, of course, pictures.
- Professional basics: What do you do? How long and how successfully have you been doing it? And, thinly veiled, can you support yourself doing it, are you looking for a helping hand or could you offer one?
- Social basics: Where do you live, who do you know, where do you vacation, and maybe even what do you drive? In effect, where do you fit in the social matrix of our community?
- Leisure basics: Hobbies, interests, passions, pastimes— anything I can fantasize doing with you? Are you devoted to anything that I have absolutely ruled out (like, say,

canoeing, which my ex pressured me into doing and at least I never have to do that again)?

- Emotional/spiritual/behavioral basics: Do you smoke, drink, or get high? Pray and, if so, how often and to whom? Take medication, see a shrink, a trainer, or an anger management coach? Are you bitter or at peace, in recovery or in treatment, warm or distant?
- Future relationship aspirations: Are you seeking a standing New Year's Eve date? Marriage, multiple sexual partners, or, God forbid, both?

Eventually you will want to fill in every one of these social blanks, and so will your potential partner. The problem is that you may feel an urgency to fill in some crucial blank immediately, before you have invested a significant amount of time and energy. Direct and early inquiry will save you time, it's true. But it will also screen out some very suitable men who give the wrong answer to one of your questions.

The problem is that we all get anxious. We've been burned, stayed in relationships too long, and feel we've ignored signs we should have heeded from day one. And we'll be damned if we will allow that to happen again. Or we believe that at this point in life we should somehow be able to read people quickly and approach men realistically. We pride ourselves on knowing what we are seeking and figure we shouldn't waste time on a man who can't go there with us.

All this is perfectly reasonable, even unarguable. It's putting it into operation that is problematic. The urge to weed out the nonstarters early convinces us to make up arbitrary lists of Red

Flags. Red Flags are traits or behaviors that, in the opinion of some women, indicate *Danger! Do Not Proceed with Relationship.* Here are examples of Red Flags used by some:

- No man who has a bad relationship with his mother.
- Or is still bitter about his ex, is too close to his ex, or has more than three of them, whatever the relationship.
- No man who is unemployed, or underemployed, or too involved with his work to make time for a relationship.
- No perennial bachelor, no alcohol abuser, road rager, or clingy phobic.
- No one whose kids need to approve his every move, or whose kids don't talk to him, or who insists your kid call before coming over.
- No man who has a steady Saturday-night date but is still calling you for Friday, or who cheated on his past wives— even though by this age he may have finally slowed down.
- No one who is anti-marriage, anti-commitment, or anti-women in general.
- And the idiosyncratic: No one who dislikes dogs, drives a jalopy, has recently had a serious health problem, doesn't believe in hiring help—or any other characteristics you've identified as a Red Flag, at least for you.

You might make romantic decisions guided by any or all of the items on this (partial, I assure you) Red Flag list. There's a good argument to be made that each is the sign of a potential problem, and if that's a problem you are trying to avoid, it's best to skip over that person. (Of course, the best way to avoid relationship problems is to stay home with your cat. Otherwise, frankly, pick your poison.)

In the early phase of dating, though, you may feel pressed to identify those potential problems as soon as possible, for all the soul-sparing, time-saving reasons we discussed earlier. That urgency works against you. It sets you up to abandon conversation in favor of interrogation, at least in the eyes of the man across the table.

As one attractive, decent, divorced architect described it, "I had at least a dozen or more first dates and the women were pretty much alike. They all wanted my story—why was I separated, what happened. They want past history and they inquired about my future plans. I mean, some are direct and some are creative, but they nearly all want to know, right away. When I'm dating, I'm much more in the now. I want a woman to suggest some activity that she and I could engage in that would be fun."

Another man seconded him. "Single women are cautious and pressing. The early date questions all seemed to communicate, 'You're a guy. So what screwy thing are you about?' Maybe, given some of their experiences, I could understand their attitude. But I didn't like it."

Here's the thinking of a third, a remarkably handsome businessman, devoted father, and dumbfounded divorcé. Divorce rocked him because he absolutely believed in lifetime commitment, for better or for worse. "I swallowed the horse pill of my marriage and decided to keep on going. My wife decided not." Despite the fact that his male friends are living vicariously, urging him to sexual conquest now that he is liberated, the specter of many women and many beds does not appeal to him. (Surely he is the one-man argument for human cloning?)

Here's something to note, though. Dating conversation has usually put him off. You may cringe at his assessment—both because of its arrogance, and because of its accuracy. He says, "I've been out on three or four dates and it's a drag. Every woman is thinking, 'This guy is great. What do I have to do to keep this going?' Then they ask probing questions trying to figure out if it's worth it for them to invest the energy. I see these intense eyes looking at me across a table, wondering, 'Are you him?' To me, it comes off as needy and creepy."

The very screening stance that so many men remark upon warily is a skill on which some women pride themselves. One single mother, who is very satisfied with her own vetting technique, offers these pointers:

"I ask pointed questions like, 'Have you been married before? Oh? Do you keep in contact with your ex-wife?' If I hear a lot of rage at the ex, I say no and move on. And if the man has never been married, that's a red light too. It means he has a commitment problem. Men have so many choices. It's so easy for a man to be married. If he hasn't, it means he doesn't want to. I'm not looking for commitment immediately, but I don't want to start out with a no.

"I'll also ask an open-ended question like, 'Tell me about your job.' I don't need to be with someone who is a gazillionaire, but I don't want to be someone's retirement plan either. I'm not looking to adopt someone.

"And I'll push a little to find out about family relationships. If someone is not talking to his kids or someone else in his family, he has an intimacy problem. It's a yellow light, for sure."

You will need to find your own comfort zone between this experienced woman's clear and pointed agenda and most men's discomfort with early interrogation. Wherever you find your personal balance, consider erring in the direction of letting things unfold. An early checklist of questions tends to screen out more than it helps you connect up. Intense early screening will probably allow you to avoid some lemons. But you'll also lose out on some surprisingly positive relationships with men who give wrong answers early on, if only because they have to work their way to the ones you would prefer to hear.

That same divorced architect commented, "Sometimes women would ask, 'Why are you going out with me?' It took me a long time to figure out what that meant, but ultimately I decided it meant, 'Are you looking for a monogamous, committed relationship?' In fact, if I told a woman that I wasn't interested in remarriage, many of them lost interest right there. The thing is, I did remarry, but at the time I was asked, I didn't feel like I could promise that I would. So if she lost interest, oh well."

That's the thing. The questions are important, but the early answers might be useless. After all, some men get good at telling you what you want to hear, whether it's true or not. One longtime bachelor confessed his strategy when asked how he presented a new woman with the fact that he'd been single for twenty years.

"Well," he said, "I can't hide it. It's a small community and everyone knows everyone else's romantic story. But if I really like a woman I might say, 'I don't know why I never remarried. I'm trying to make some changes about that.' If it's a woman I find very attractive, I might hold out that possibility. And it's not a lie at all, because at the moment I'm saying it, and looking at her,

I am thinking maybe it could happen. But so far, for one reason or another, it hasn't turned out that way."

Instead of honing your inquiry, you might learn just as much by asking little and watching carefully. Remember Yogi Berra's advice: "You can see a lot, just by looking."

You can reveal a lot too, but in a thoughtful and self-aware way. Disciplined presentation of self means having comfortable answers to classic dating questions and exposing some of your own less attractive features with conscious care.

Classic dating questions, like conventional job interview topics, are most efficiently addressed by telling the simple truth. But for one reason or another, the truth is not always something you might wish to reveal so early in your acquaintanceship. In that case, you'll need to be prepared with an answer you can be comfortable with, an answer that finesses the truth just enough that you can breathe easy.

It's really no different from the preparation you'd make for a job interview. You walk in with an imperfect résumé and you know the interviewer is likely to ask about that long unemployed period. So you work up a decent explanation. Then, if the question comes up, you're ready. If it doesn't come up, so much the better.

Here are some common dating questions in answer to which some women find that the flat-out truth could be improved upon.

1. How old are you? (Or some version of fishing for your age, like "I don't usually meet a young woman like you in this bar," or "What year did you say you graduated?")

    It's best to decide how you'll handle the age question going in, because every Internet site asks for it and your dates are very likely to inquire also. The truth works well, though lies work too if they are within a reasonable range of the truth. Still, it's way too easy, in the Google era, to discover the truth, so a specific lie is less successful these days. If you want to dodge the whole question, you can refuse to answer. You might try:

A direct, "I don't tell my age." Delivered with a smile, but still firmly delivered. This irritates some who either disapprove or don't like to take no for an answer. This type of person will push. The rest will respect your boundary and won't ask again—for a date or two.

A light remark like, "I don't reveal anything with numbers—age, weight, or income. Do you?"

A gentle push back like, "Hey, I'll tell you my age if you'll tell me how much you make?"

Or, perhaps best of all if you can deliver it well, try the following dialogue:

> He: How old are you?
> You (*leaning forward*): Can you keep a secret?
> He: Sure.
> You: So can I.

2. How old do you think I am?

Yes, there are still people asking this geeky question. You know enough to simply smile and, if forced, respond with something similarly jejeune like "Old enough to know what you're doing?" Har har har.

3. Do you hate men?

> Right answer? "Sometimes. But not often."
>
> True answer? Waaay too long to go into.

4. So, what happened in your marriage? What led to the divorce?

No one can supply your best right answer here, but it's wise to give this some serious thought before your first coffee date. You will eventually be asked, and your answer will have as much impact on you as it has on a prospective suitor.

A bald version of the truth ("He left me for a younger woman." "He was cheating for years and I finally threw him out." "He's an alcoholic loser and it took me all this time to get the strength to walk away." "He was mean and depressed and I couldn't stand being married to him anymore." "He lost his job and I couldn't see myself supporting him forever.") tends to rachet up the emotional intimacy of the conversation beyond what's comfortable for early dating.

A vague cliché ("We grew apart." "It was both our faults." "It just wasn't working anymore.") will satisfy some, at least temporarily. At the least it's a signal that you don't want to get into your personal history at this point, and many will honor your reserve. But you will probably need a more substantive answer should the relationship develop. If he never asks again, he is far too incurious about you.

Sometimes the most suitable thing you can say in answer to the question "What happened to your marriage?" is "I don't know. Not fully. I'm still working on that." Then make sure you work on it.

5. Are you seeing anyone?

This should be an easy question to answer truthfully, but it turns out there are circumstances in which it's not. You might not want a new man to know just how little competition he has. On the other hand, you might be seeing someone quite regularly, but you want to keep your options open. Both situations call for a lie, yet lying is not necessarily something to which we all wish to stoop, just for the sake of a date.

Decide for yourself, of course. But do keep in mind that the fuzzy generality, "I'm dating, but no one serious," covers a multitude of arrangements. One savvy dater learned to counter this vague response with a more specific question of her own: "Is there anyone who expects to see you on Saturday night?" Now, that's a considerably tougher inquiry to tap dance around.

Here's a response, though, with which another woman countered when she didn't want to 'fess up that she had a regular boyfriend, but that didn't stop her from interviewing others. When asked about her relationship status, she answered: "I am in negotiation, but I am not under agreement." Well, at least it's something to say.

6. How many men have you slept with besides your husband?

Out of bounds. Maybe forever. Draw the privacy line and hold fast.

7. What are you looking for?

Good answers include "a friend," "love," "a good time," "a companion," "a long fascinating conversation," or "I really don't have a list" (even though you probably do).

Off-putting answers are those that reflect poorly on your experiences with men: "one honest guy," "anyone not a jerk," "a grown-up, if possible."

8. What would your ex (or your deceased husband) say about you? How would he describe you?

Not everyone gets this creative or this direct, but it is a pretty interesting question. You might even consider answering this one honestly for yourself. There's probably something to learn in it.

You will also want to be disciplined in your presentation of self by exposing your own less attractive features—your yo-yo dieting, say, or your career exhaustion, or your son's drug history—later than you might with a new girlfriend. It simply takes you and a new man longer to develop enough of an emotional bond to bear the freight.

There are lots of reasons for this different reaction—some obvious, some not so. But the bottom line is this: A woman who is especially unguarded might meet another woman at a party and end up confiding every homicidal impulse she's ever had toward the ex-husband who takes the kids on swell vacations while "forgetting" alimony payments. These new friends will understand each other perfectly and may even end up trying on each other's shoes. But tell a man with whom you've had three dates this same tale of fury and, somewhere behind his pleasant social support, there is apt to be a cringe.

What may be intended as open and frank revelation sounds, to many men, like pure trouble—especially early on in a dating relationship. "The biggest turn-off to me," said one fifty-five-year-old divorced actor, "is when I hear about how miserably a woman's ex is affecting her life. If they are arguing about money or the kids or he didn't make a payment, or they have some ugly confrontation—well, it's a horrible thing for the woman that is totally understandable, but then she becomes obsessed with it. I really don't want to talk about that all the time."

Another longer-divorced male concurred. "Once the ex enters our relationship, because she starts confiding in me for a guy's point of view or something, I know it will be hard for me to be closer to that woman. I don't know how to solve those problems and I don't want all that ugliness in my life. I think many women feel the same about men who complain all the time about their ex-wives. But they don't always hear themselves."

A third, solvent, much-courted widower with hair, said it flat-out. "Women want to talk about their kids, their grandchildren, and the exes. It's just plain *boring*."

Just because your behavior makes a man uncomfortable, that certainly doesn't mean you should change it. You might decide, simply, this is you and he can take it or leave it. But it would help you to be forewarned about his discomfort.

*   *   *

In the end though, neither your social résumé nor his should have to be extracted. If you let things unfold a bit and pay careful attention, important information will be gradually revealed. Along the way, you will be furthering your connection by pursuing conversational common ground. Even there it helps to be aware of a few hidden land mines.

In the best of circumstances, finding safe common ground is blessedly easy. If, for example, you met through a shared interest, you can presume an overlap that creates instant warmth:

> He started talking to me on the art tour. I noticed immediately that he was attractive, affable, and he was wearing Paul Smith socks. We immediately buddied up and talked about collections like we'd been comparing ideas forever.

> We met on a blind date, but I knew from my friend that he was a runner and I have just started training for my first marathon. I decided to pick his brain for training ideas.

> I'll mention some headline—just kind of throw it out there, because I love city politics. A woman doesn't have to be interested for me to like her, but if she is, that's a great date to me.

Of course, when your turfs so obviously overlap, you don't need much guidance. But searching for common threads can be grounds to tread lightly. For example, a brief discussion of your relationship to the person who fixed you up is expected. But you can't go a great conversational distance regarding shared acquaintances, because you can't trust each other well enough to enjoy a satisfying gossip about them.

Too, who-do-we-know-in-common is a natural attempt to place a stranger into some familiar social matrix. If it turns out that this Internet date plays golf with your college roommate, or lives next door to your dentist, you will both certainly feel more connected. (A feeling that, by the way, you may or may not enjoy.) But it can be awkward too, if you or your date feel yourselves to be weighed and measured in the process of discovering common bonds.

"Who do you know, where do you live, what do you do?" are all customary conversational connectors, and certainly they will come up unless you decide to be deliberately interesting and so avoid them. Just understand (of course you do) that commonplace as these questions are, they are also codes for income level and social status.

There's nothing wrong with being curious about either, and you will definitely want to discover these social definers somewhere down the road. But it's sexier and more interesting, at least at first, to show him the person behind your social status, or to try to discover the person behind his. Besides, rich guys want to tell you about their toys, but they like to pretend that's not why you're interested, and struggling guys feel easily judged and inadequate, waiting defensively for you to pass them shallowly by. It's therefore safer, on early dates, to tiptoe around status measurement.

He will certainly also be measuring your own social standing, and you'll need to decide how you want to present that piece of your own résumé. Some women are frank realists, as was this seventy-five-year-old woman who described how she attracted her older lover: "He took one look at the fact that I still wear a size six and I have my own purse and he fell instantly in love."

Other women are less comfortable being desired for something other than their personal appeal. One said, "I don't let any man see my house or meet my friends until I think it's going to be serious, because I don't want any guy who is going to climb a social ladder on my back." There's no one right attitude, but it's good to know your own sensitivities and cater to them accordingly.

If conversations about the people whom you know in common have their delicate spots, talk about your dating experiences can unwittingly cast you in an unflattering light too. Dating war stories are an easy conversational topic, especially if this date is the result of an Internet meeting or dating service matchup. In the gap after Hello and Did you have any trouble recognizing me, finding the place, with the traffic—one or both of you might end up comparing notes about your experiences on eHarmony.

You are funny, you are interesting, and your stories always make your girlfriends laugh. But a word of caution. Sometimes men hear them differently. They may hear . . . bitterness. "Women tend to talk about their wacky dates, about how hard it is to meet a normal guy. I'm sure it's all true—but it's part of what makes them seem all alike and needy," one widower said frankly.

He was most straightforward about it, but many men touched on the same sentiment. Just as you are sensitive to remarks that tip you off to a man who doesn't appear to like women, men are vigilant about a woman who appears angry with or disappointed by men. Funny dating stories sometimes have a sour ring to a male ear.

With all this, you might decide to tell whatever stories you like and if a guy doesn't get the joke, so be it. No one can dictate what you should talk about, what part of your social résumé to reveal and what part to be more discreet about, what questions to ask early and which to skip forever. But, as with all communication, it's good to be aware not simply of the message you are sending, but of the one that is being received.

Let's assume that, whatever guidelines you've established for yourself, something is working. Somehow, whether at first sight and who-cares-what-you-talked-about, or over the crème brûlée, whether through the course of several dinners and movies and what-have-yous or just after the third drink you shared on the night you met, whatever it took—a connection has been established. If so, and maybe sooner than you would have believed, you are up to the next question: "Now that we've established common ground, are we moving to a common bed?"

Care to Come In?

A sixty-one-year-old art therapist relates this experience: "Yesterday I shared an elevator in my office building with a pleasant-faced man I had seen in the elevator before but never spoken to. As we exited, he smiled at me and said, 'Excuse me. I wonder if you would be interested in having sex with me?' 'Thanks so much for asking,' I said, 'but I really don't think so.' We went on our separate ways. Then I tried to beat myself up for the 'thanks so much for asking.' I mean, is that any way to talk to a pervert? But I didn't get very far. The truth is, that little exchange pumped me up for two days."

You might believe you will never actually get naked again—because nobody will be interested enough to ask. Women over sixty, over fifty—hey, over forty—talk about becoming sexually invisible to men and suffering for it. And it is true that, as anonymous sexual icons merely strolling down the street, most older women are not the stuff of private fantasy. (With, say, Sophia Loren as the notable and enduring exception.)

But once a connection is established over a drink, a date, or even, apparently, an elevator ride, the question of sex is on the table. It is a question fraught with possible consequence, which is why so many of us choose not to think it through at all. We sometimes prefer blindly leaping and making do with wherever we land. On the other hand, there are some considerations that will help you establish a thoughtful sexual policy for fun and possible profit.

When you return to romantic life, you will probably confront common sexual decision points: when to, how to, how safely to, and, finally, what to expect afterward. These concerns might all be vaguely familiar to you from the period before your marriage or whenever you last remember dating. And some of it—or to some women, all of it—might strike you as entirely new.

There is no right rule for how long to wait before sleeping with a man, though that won't stop you from trying to establish one for yourself. It's so easy to seek out a rule that will medicate your worry—"Is this too soon? Too late? What will he think of me, either way?" And then, in irritated defiance, "Who the hell cares what he thinks? What do *I* think?" Which will probably bring you full circle back to "Is this too soon? Too late?" And so on.

Aauugghh. Dating has returned you to the crazy insecurities of your youth. But it might only be a temporary visit. Remind yourself of what you've learned since then:

• Sexual decision making, like sex itself, is an imperfect art at best. Any decision you make could be flawed—but not fatally.

- Men have their own version of sexual angst. When it comes to dating, there's no free lunch.

- A relationship progresses because of the strength of its con-nective tissue. And sex is only one small part of that. His unfulfilled desire for sex will keep him calling for a little bit, though probably not forever. Satisfying your mutual desire for sex will not ensure that he calls again, nor will it guarantee that he will drop you with a thud. That decision rests on many other factors.

In the end you will decide to sleep with a new partner when you are sexually interested enough to proceed and comfortable enough to take your clothes off. For sure you might occasionally regret that decision. Ultimately you might feel you slept with him too soon, or, looking back, you might wish you hadn't missed a terrific op-portunity. Even recognizing this, you can still have confidence in your next decision, because you've come to realize that a great life includes many grand mistakes. You make yours with a smile.

Well, with a smile . . . eventually. If you are returning to ro-mantic life after decades with one man, a new partner can be an incredibly alien experience. First there is the simple shock of being physically naked in front of a new lover. Then there is the strangeness of his fresh body, which is longer or rounder or hairier than the one to which you've been accustomed. Plus it smells different. Not bad, certainly. But maybe . . . foreign.

Get past the shock of his body and your own, naked somehow under the same sheet, and then there's the whole process of who does what to whom when. Maybe this is like riding a bicycle, but this bicycle is built for two and the sheer coordination can be pretty damn awkward at first.

The bottom line—*just do it*—may contain a core of truth: You will get better at this, and more relaxed too, with practice. But there are some confidence-building strategies that might help. For one thing, you can jump-start your self-confidence by reconnecting with your own body before you try it out with someone else's. You might find that personal sexual reawakening takes a little concentrated effort, because marriage, motherhood, or menopause have temporarily disconnected your sexual circuits.

In fact, for the last years, or even decades, you may have been all head—sprinting day after day through the family/job treadmill, balancing coupons against a family budget, thinking, organizing, crossing chores off long to-do lists. Or you may have been mostly heart—succoring your children, supporting your husband, remembering your mother-in-law's birthday. Whether head or heart or, more likely, a balance of both, your body could well have taken last place in the competition for your attention.

Now here you are, considering a return to romantic life where your body's needs, urges, and contours are central to the experience. You just might have to reintroduce yourself. If that's the case (and it's hard to imagine that it wouldn't be, at least to some degree), here's what might help.

- The gym: Okay, I know, it's the panacea for nearly everything and you are tired of hearing it. But the thing is, it *is* the panacea for nearly everything, or at least all the things we're talking about right now.
- A spa: Go for a week. Go for a day. Then go again, as often as your budget can bear. Get a massage. A scrub. An absurdly expensive, makes-no-rational-sense treatment, like

one with crushed grape stems or mango particles. This is a full-body experience. No, it won't magically make you rip your clothes off the first time you have to make love to a stranger. But it will inch you closer.

- Your gynecologist: Your doctor is the proper person to introduce you to the wonders of various estrogen creams, patches, hormone treatments, tinctures of testosterone, and/or natural supplements—some of which might be sexual enhancements for you. Don't let shyness deprive you of this resource. Believe me, your doctor has heard it all before. And don't feel like you have to have a prospective partner before you ask these questions. Sometimes it's best to reconnect with your own body before anyone else does.

- High heels and lingerie: This girly-girl stuff might not be your style. But then again, you might want to experiment with your style at this moment. Anyway, don't close yourself off to it. Pumps that make your calves look tight and a bra with more lace than you needed when you were the Girl Scout Mother can have an unexpectedly positive impact on your own libido.

- Sex toys: Did you know there are books written just to stimulate the female sexual fantasy (we prefer a plot) and equipment to arouse and satisfy female desire? You might have limited yourself to the inspiration your husband could supply during the years of your relationship. But hey—you're single now.

- And, of course, a lover: In the next chapter we'll talk about the confidence-building possibilities of a sexual mentor. For now, remember, you don't have to be perfectly poised before you get naked again. In fact, you can tell a new partner how nervous you are, ask to have the lights off, tell him you need reassurance, hide under the covers, or whatever else gets you past those first naked moments. Frankly, there's a good chance he won't mind at all. At worst, he'll take it as a challenge and try to help you relax. At best, he'll be relieved. At least he's not alone in his anxiety.

Some women newly turned single make a sexual decision first, then review the world wide-eyed to discover a possible partner. You test yourself with a lover, endure some awkwardness, and finally find your comfort zone. A freshly divorced middle school teacher described this sexual strategy:

"By the time I got through all my firsts—the drink dates and e-mail encounters—I had already decided it was time to have a sexual experience. So I was ready when the chance presented itself. I met him in a bar. He seemed to me to be an opportunity, partly because it was nothing but sexual. He was younger, attractive, just looking for a drink and to get laid. And I wasn't interested yet in having a relationship.

"We met at random intervals for months. I did not fall in love, but I was disappointed anyway. I wanted an affair and a playmate and he wasn't interested in any of that. He just wanted drinks and sex. He's an example of that whole new generational thing of the hookup, which generally involves a lot of alcohol. It's all about the alcohol really, because you have to numb yourself to loosen your inhibitions.

"I did stop feeling good with him eventually, so I ended it. But he took me a step forward. Somehow it gave me a whole new identity and I went, in my own mind, from dumped middle-aged wife to dating person. Wow. Pretty good."

Other women echo this same theme: The decision to become sexually alive precedes the discovery of a partner with whom to experience the awakening. "I wanted to have sex again before I die," one woman stated flatly. "And I realized that if I wanted to, I might have to hunt it down, because outwardly I do not come off as your typical sex kitten."

Another repeated that same funny, determined attitude. "It was the terrorist idea that got me," she said. "I broke up with my boyfriend of fifteen years right after 9/11 and I had this constant feeling that time was running out. Who knows when another attack could come and screw up our lives forever? I kept thinking, 'I've got to have sex before they strike.' It was a crazy thought, but it did get me past a lot of shyness."

Whatever motivates your own decision making, sexual determination can get you into some man's bed. That doesn't mean you'll necessarily be happy once you get there, and that's okay too.

Rona remembered her first post-divorce sexual encounter clearly, even though she is now two years into her second marriage. "But," she says, "some awkward life moments do not fade with time. My first attempt at a sexual experience after my marriage broke up was kind of . . . medicinal. He was someone's single relative. After we met, he invited me to New York for the weekend, and I decided it was a prospect I should pursue.

"It felt very strange to me because I had done the whole thing so often with my husband—you know, go out, stroll around, put on the hotel robe to take a nap before dinner. At some point in the robe time, I thought, 'Let's get this over with.' And we did. I guess it was fine, but when I woke up I just wanted to *go home*. I had already decided this wasn't going to be a relation-ship. So it felt fake. I just wanted to go home and see my kids and feel . . . real."

Rona's second thoughts are not uncommon. Other women reported similar experiences: "I had a few times where I got asked into someone's bed, got as far as taking off my clothes, and then sat up and left, because this just didn't feel right."

Sometimes your body has second thoughts for you:

Here was a man I had been fantasizing about for months, but when he finally made a move I just dried up instantly. My mind was certainly willing, but somehow you couldn't get a penis in me with a pliers.

We are still together and we can laugh now about my attack of first-night diarrhea. That did put a damper on things for a few hours.

It was a personal low, that's for sure. We were in a glamor-ous hotel out of town, made love, fell asleep, and let me tell you, I couldn't get over myself in this sexy setting. I have been your bake sale, car pool mom for the last hundred years of my life and here I was, naked under three-hundred-thread-count sheets with a French lover. Total mental high five, you know?

Anyway, I woke up in the middle of the night and walked naked to the bathroom to pee. On the way, for some reason I passed out on the floor. Too much to drink earlier, I guess. The truth is, I'm not much of a drinker, but I was trying to keep up. Anyway I was naked, unconscious on the floor, and I came to after a second and projectile-vomited all over myself. I opened my eyes and there he was, looking down at me to see if he should call 911.

He was actually pretty great. Cleaned me up, got me back to bed, and, I guess because he's French, and we were both awake anyway, we had sex again. But in the morning, when I had to recall what I must have looked like naked in the pool of vomit, well . . . I just kept telling myself, it's all uphill from here, right?

Your own first sexual experiences might be sublime or similarly awkward, but they will likely follow a decision on your part to get in the sexual net game. If you make that decision with a practice partner—a sexual mentor—you are in one particular kind of situation. We'll discuss that relationship in the next chapter. If, on the other hand, you get sexually involved with a man who is something other than an icebreaking opportunity or a sexual hookup, you have entered that delicate relationship area: who-means-what-owes-what-expects-what-from-whom?

Here are some male perspectives on the sexual questions of when and what's it all mean:

They all want to jump into bed. They say to themselves, "This is a handsome, well-to-do, separated man and I should connect with him quickly before someone else does." On the first date, we would meet someplace casual. On the second date, they'd ask me to pick them up. This was not always some kind of sexual indication, but it usually was. Then, when I took them home, they would invite me in. I'm pretty reserved and that was kind of awkward for me, you know, where to sit, whether to make a move. But there was usually no expectation on her part of any kind of courtship. I was pretty cautious, though. Because really, after my breakup I was just out to have fun, and once you have sex there are expectations.

My male friends put the most pressure on me. I was the single one now and they were all long married. They liked to imagine me having sex three nights a week with a different woman every night and they joked with me about it. I could have gone that route, I guess, if I had wanted to, because there are plenty of women around. But it's not me and I didn't feel comfortable.

Actually the woman I ended up with was more hesitant than most. She seemed to know that I was in the newly single stage and she told me frankly that she thought I wasn't ready to get involved. She made me wait six dates before we became lovers and that actually made us more connected, more affectionate with each other.

I'm too old to want to have sex with every girl I have a second date with. Sometimes I just want them there as a date. But if I do want to have sex, I make some sort of physical advance. If she's receptive, great. If she's not, I move on.

In my younger years, I had fun sex with women who seemed happy to have fun sex with me. No strings. But now the women I'm with are all over fifty and fun sex doesn't seem to work out anymore. No matter how clearly I tell them up front—and I do tell them—that I don't want a committed relationship, I can't get them to believe me. They say it's fine, but pretty quickly it's not fine. She starts the "how do you feel, where is this relationship going?" conversation. When I say it's not going anywhere, it's fine where it is, the women get really angry with me. I can't find a way around raising a woman's expectations and then hurting her, except maybe no sex at all.

Whether or not women do want to jump into bed, they certainly feel that men expect them to be willing to. Many describe the same early sexual pressure, though they tend to experience it originating from male expectation rather than their own.

"All men approach me sexually, pretty much on the first or second date," said one very social, divorced interior designer. How? "They say so, flat-out. They say 'I want to sleep with you,' 'I want to make love to you,' 'I want to have sex with you,' or 'I want to fuck you'—depending on the man. Or they introduce a lot of sexual flirting. They'll say, 'You're gorgeous,' which I am not. Or 'You have a great body.' It's a signal, that's all.

"I know how to say no. I might say 'not yet' or 'it's too soon for me' or something like that. Or just plain flat-out no. It doesn't call for a story. And men don't mind hearing no, they're used to it. Every one of them is going to try for sex, as a pleasant addition to the night's recreation. But they are grown-ups and they've heard no before. They're just trying. Frankly, it's harder for me to say no to a date or a dance, because that could hurt someone's feelings. And, of course, sometimes I say yes."

Whatever got you into that bed—whether it was the pressure of his sexual expectation or your own arousal, the desire to be closer to him, great lingerie that shouldn't go to waste, or just a hell of a lot to drink—once you are there, things change. One of the things that makes dating so emotionally hazardous to women is that sex provokes emotional attachment, even when we are old enough to know better.

You might be the exception to this general rule, or the shell-shocked year following your divorce might prove to be the exception to a lifetime's habit of attachment. Some men, too, fall in love when they fall into bed, even if most do not. Whatever the exceptions, here is the general principle: Women frequently experience powerful feelings of attachment after sexual intimacy.

It's hormonal, or socially conditioned, hardwired or adapted through evolutionary need. Or some or all of the above. Whatever the cause, the effect is the same. We have an unfortunate tendency to translate sex into love, pretty much from the moment of the post-coital cuddle.

If this is not true for you, if you've outgrown it or learned to defend against it, great. You will be less likely to distort sexual intimacy into emotional commitment. Sexual intimacy may or may not evolve into emotional commitment, or you might decide to delay the sex until you feel confident of the emotional commitment. But you will not confuse one with the other.

If you can keep these sane and separate, God bless you. The rest of us are still wildly vulnerable—yes, at forty or fifty, yes, at sixty, yes, at seventy-five. This emotional longing, this post-sexual gush of attachment, appears to occur independent of maturity or reason. We can learn to recognize it, though, to identify it for the romantic longing that it is.

We can come to understand that we sometimes get into bed for the sex and get out of bed expecting a relationship, and that *expecting doesn't make it so. But it hurts just as much all the same.*

One thing that does change now that we're older is that we've learned to keep those wishes and expectations to ourselves (and sometimes even, sadly, from ourselves, in an effort to pretend that something doesn't hurt just because we wish it didn't). We practice our own version of Don't Ask, Don't Tell, and sometimes make up stories to fill in the silence. Here's how one man describes it from his point of view:

> When I was dating, I felt perfectly entitled to see more than one woman. After all, I hadn't promised anyone anything. I usually was seeing more than one woman and sleeping with more than one woman. I never lied about it, but I didn't make an announcement. Most women never asked, so I didn't discuss it. I mean, what woman wants to hear that?
>
> If it did come up, though, I was honest and said I was dating. To me, *dating* implies *sleeping with*. It's just a polite way to put it. I was being tactful. But maybe with a slanted picture. If a woman asked directly, "Are you dating a lot?" I might say, "Not much. I'm just getting started." And that wasn't exactly true. I spun it, especially if I was interested in her.

None of this is meant to suggest for a second that only men shape the truth to suit their needs, while women are open and forthright. (Though to hear us complain, you might think that was the case.) You yourself might spin a truth if, for example, you are trying to do that perp walk of simultaneously having a boyfriend and looking around for a better one. A new prospect asks if you are seeing someone and you finesse your way across no, so as to hold yourself open for a fresh possibility. Truth twisting is not gender-specific.

Nor are denial, avoidance, or rationalization—that trifecta of mental dodges by which perfectly mature adults learn to ignore the emotional and sexual health conundrum of multiple partners. Both men and women hope their partners (if not themselves) are sexually exclusive and safe. And both men and women frequently act as if wishing would make it so.

Safe sex—that is, sex with a condom until your relationship is reliably sexually exclusive and you've both been tested—is something we begin to browbeat into our children by the time they've turned twelve. And we firmly believe in it—for them. As for ourselves, well, we talk the talk but that's often as far as it goes.

"I do more worrying about safe sex than practicing it," one female physician admitted. She could have been speaking for a legion of other women. Partly because she, like you, had come out of a long-term relationship where remembering to have sex at all was the issue and the safety of sex was thought to be irrelevant, she felt awkward even addressing the safe-sex question with a new lover.

"It's like that irrational sense that you can have sex with a man but borrowing his toothbrush feels too intimate. The whole question of safe sex was very unnerving for me. I knew I was supposed to have a condom but I relied on the guy in the beginning because I was used to that from dating thirty years ago. I am a doctor and I know what I am supposed to do, but I didn't always do it."

Frank sexual discussion with a man who might not yet know your middle name can be embarrassing. Some women handle that awkwardness by rationalizing away any need for such a discussion. "I've made it up in my mind that I don't need condoms because none of the men I've been with are IV drug users or bisexual," said one art director in a breathtaking dismissal of the realities of sexually transmitted diseases.

Other men and women are less dismissive, but not necessarily more effective in their approach to the problem. "I make a nod in the direction of safe sex," said an active, athletic fifty-five-year-old divorcée who has some dating experience under her belt. "This year I broke off a nine-year relationship, and I really didn't want to have to deal with the whole safe-sex thing again. But I know I should, so I kind of half deal with it. You know, I start a sort of semi-stupid conversation that goes, 'Uh, I don't have anything—do you?' It's not scientifically safe, but it makes me feel better and so far I'm still healthy."

Men will sometimes use condoms, though several reserve their use for side affairs they are having outside their relationship. ("I practice serial monogamy," one bachelor explains. "But sometimes I slip.") One recently divorced engineer spoke about his reliance on condoms when he felt himself to be casually involved in an affair, especially with a married woman. "There are so many unhappy forty- and fifty-year-old women who are dying to have sex with a nice guy. I am a nice, safe, discreet affair, complete with condom."

Some realistic women take a firm and self-protective stance and make a strict condom policy a serious priority. But others feel more comfortable establishing a middle ground, where conversation and a sense of familiarity stand in for commitment to a condom.

One shared her approach: "I've been tested and I ask if a potential partner has been. I only date one man at a time and I try to assess a partner's level of experience and therefore risk. I think

that makes me pretty vigilant." Of course, only a condom quali-
fies as vigilant, and, as noted earlier, men have been known to
minimize their other sexual activity for one reason or another.
But conversation and character assessment are probably better
than nothing.

Many men prefer a general sexual risk assessment over condoms too, because so many men (and not a few women) really
don't like the feel of condoms and are just plain unwilling to use
them. One divorced real estate guy gave this chillingly honest
recounting of his approach to safe sex: "If a woman asks me to
use a condom, I totally respect her feelings. But I won't have sex
with her. I just move on to a woman who doesn't care, because
why should I have sex that won't feel good when I can have sex
that does?"

Why indeed?

Other men were equally emphatic, if perhaps a bit less cold.
Said one retired widower, "These days I talk about safe sex first,
and I'm concerned to know someone really well and get a sense
of her background, because I want to feel there's not much risk
of disease. But I've learned that all of life is a risk, one way or
another. I try to minimize the risk, of course, but I'm willing to
take some. I'm not willing to use a condom because, frankly, I
just can't perform if I do."

Which brings us to performance—his, yours, and ultimately
a couple's.

If the female sexual road is dangerous because it leads straight
to the heart, the male sexual road has its own perils, because it
raises the question of sexual performance. Sometimes, unfortunately, that's all it raises.

The lover over fifty is different from that same man as a lover at twenty. When he's seventy, he's different still. Those biological changes are predictable—softer, less dependable erections, elusive orgasms, fewer sexual fantasies and desires—though their pace varies for every individual man. A man's reaction to those changes, however, is less predictable, and that reaction will affect your love affair as much as the changes themselves.

The most common reactions are anxiety ("Oh my God, I can't get it up. Will she laugh? Will she tell? Will she leave?") and a sense of loss with its accompanying sadness. Some men take that anxiety and loss to an extreme and abandon sex forever—which may be the unspoken issue with that nice man you've been dating for six months who never tries to get more intimate than a kiss good night.

Others put the responsibility for their diminishing sexual arousal on aging female partners, believing firmly (at least something is firm) that with a younger, riper woman their own orgasm delays and erection disappointments would disappear. Overheard on Comedy Central:

"Daddy, what's Viagra?"

"Viagra is a pill that Daddy has to take because Mommy is getting old."

There's some painful truth to that sexist joke. A newer, fresher, more visually stimulating partner often will give a man a stronger erection, or make it easier for him to orgasm initially, at least temporarily, until she's no longer new. Eventually, though, even hotter sex becomes habitual, and that man has to look elsewhere for new stimulation.

It's a waste of energy to hate this guy for looking right through you and moving from one thirty-five-year-old to the next. For one thing, you might enjoy a thirty-five-year-old yourself from time to time.

Some women are very frank about their preference for a younger lover. "I'm sixty," said one widow, "but I relate better to men who are forty-five to fifty-five. By the time a man gets to be sixty-five, he's tired. His sex drive drops way off, and that leads to some uncomfortable moments. I'm interested in a man over sixty-five for his investment advice, but for sex I'm looking elsewhere."

She's not alone in her sexual assessment. As one fifty-six-year-old salon owner said of her ten-years-younger boyfriend, "I don't think he and I could be a settled relationship ever, but at least I don't have to put up with any penile dementia." Younger men are less likely to suffer from penile dementia, and certainly partnering with one is a solution to a woman's disappointment with diminished male sexual capacity. And, just as not all women date younger men but some do, not all men date very young women, but some do.

In addition, not all men respond to the changes in their sexuality with defensiveness, denial, or blame, just as not all women respond to their own aging bodies with depression and anxiety. But many of us, male and female, pass through those negative stages before we make peace. Men and women can come to view their aging bodies with acceptance and to recognize their sexual changes as just that—a change over time, rather than simply as a loss.

Those alterations can make men slower, more sensual lovers and can turn women into franker, more expressive partners. True, sexual mechanics are different at forty and then different again at sixty, but *different* is not necessarily a synonym for *worse*. A slower, more sensitive man, who is making love to a woman able to express her desires openly, can experience a level of sexual satisfaction beyond what he felt when he could come twice a day at twenty and be ready for more. But he has to stop comparing himself with what he was and appreciate who he has become. That's a process in and of itself.

The giving and receiving of physical pleasure is available to you with old lovers, young lovers, impotent lovers and erect ones, hard pounders and back strokers. The key to satisfaction is in the emotional connection between you and your lover and in how much you two are willing and able to communicate about your sexual relationship. But hey, when was that conversation ever easy, no matter what your age?

Resuming romantic life, most of us just hope we'll be able to take off our clothes, jump into sex, and it'll all work great. And it might. But frequently that takes some tinkering. Frank discussion, whether of sexual preferences or of the vagaries of older bodies in bed, is a tough aspect of getting naked again.

Only one other topic might be equally touchy: money.

I'll Get That

In romantic relationships, sex and money have significant power and not dissimilar dynamics. Both impact whom you'll find attractive and who might be drawn to you. Both are highly intimate aspects of life, making it likely that your communication on these subjects will be coded rather than direct, especially early in a relationship. And both sexual and financial choices are constrained by the same moral precept, namely, what's acceptable is whatever occurs between two consenting adults that does not harm others.

Just as in sexual matters, though, proper financial behavior between consenting adults is not an easy thing on which to agree. That makes the romantic question of who spends what on whom more complicated than it might otherwise appear to be. Just as matched expectations make sexual relationships more satisfying, parallel financial expectations make for easier partnerships. And, as in sexual relationships—since when have male and female expectations ever perfectly matched?

Besides, you've been out of the game for a considerable period of time. How do you even know what to expect financially these days, whether from a date or a lover? Well, some of it is what you've been taught to expect:

> In my generation, in my social group, really in every context that I know how to think of it, men pick up the check. He pays, and I cook from time to time to reciprocate. And also, I guess, to show him that I do womanly nurturing things. And I like to do them. That hasn't changed in my world since I was seventeen and I couldn't imagine that any man I date would feel comfortable changing those financial arrangements now.

> When my husband died he left me a five-million-dollar insurance policy and that changed my whole financial world. But I would never spend a penny of that on a man I dated. Men pay for dates because it's their role. He's the guy. You need to let him be the man.

Sometimes we learn what to expect only once we get out into the dating world:

> I've been on over a dozen coffee dates with men I've met on an Internet dating site. I've learned that most men expect you

to pay for your own coffee on those dates. It always feels a little cheap to me, which is maybe why I haven't been nuts about any of the guys. But I can understand it too. These meetings get expensive if you are doing a lot of them. And I probably make as much money as the men I'm meeting. So it makes sense to pay my share. Makes sense, feels yucky.

If it's a poor guy, we split it. If it's a rich guy, he pays. But men always pay for the first date. Period.

Women want you to pay, expect you to pay, and the richer the woman, the more important it seems to be to her that you do pay. I think that's all about them worrying that you are interested in them for the money. I've had women whom I'd taken to dinner who were about to drive away in a BMW turn around to me to take a dollar to tip the valet. I'm a gentleman, so I give it to them.

Men always pay for the first date. That's how they signal that this is a date and not a mere platonic exchange of ideas. And I let them pay, when I'm romantically interested. If there is no sexual charge, I'll probably insist on paying my half. That's how I signal, "This ain't happenin'." It doesn't work every time, but often enough.

Sometimes those coded financial messages are at cross purposes:

She says: "I always offer to split a check with a man in our first dates. I wish he wouldn't take it, but usually he does."

He says: "I try to handle money like it's relationship nuclear waste. You just gotta be careful because you never know. You know how sometimes when you hold a door for a woman, it bugs them, and sometimes they love it? Money is the same thing. If she says nothing, I pick up the check for the date. If she offers, I take it. I try to do whatever seems important to her, because women are touchy and I'm never sure what they will take as disrespectful."

Sometimes the check becomes a personality test: "In the beginning, the men I date pay. Later on, I'll do my share. But I already know that I'm loving and giving. I need to know how giving they are."

And some tests you'll fail no matter what: "When I date, usually the men pay. But I'm open to the alternative. I had one relationship with a guy who was really cheap—didn't want to pay for a thing. I was comfortable with that, really questioned why I thought men had to pay. I don't believe I'm entitled to that or deserve it or something. It's just what I've been used to. I was willing to change, to look at myself. But then he broke up with me—he decided I was too expensive."

Maybe there is no one right rule, but there is enough financial consensus to guide you until you have settled into a comfortable sense of your own expectations. Initially,

—the person who does the inviting pays (so if you called to mention your extra theater tickets, he is your guest),
—*unless he insists on paying*, in which case he is probably signaling his romantic (versus platonic) interest. You should respond according to the message you want to send back.

There's no need for you to follow this rule. If you prefer absolute financial parity from the outset (and you might, because you've learned that there is a delicious sense of power that comes with being the one who picks up the check), then pay your own way or pay his too. If he's not comfortable, so be it.

If, on the other hand, *the man pays* is a rule etched indelibly on your psyche and you are unable or unwilling to rewrite that script, well, your indifference to the check will make your expectations clear from the outset. You will be best off with a man whose psyche is carved in a matching outline.

And what if you are trying, with this return to the courtship game, to rewrite your own set of financial rules? Like any transformation, with concentrated effort that can be achieved. You'll need a clear direction, commitment, and, if possible, a coach.

Julie, an architecture critic and art history professor, resolved to do just that after her divorce. "I was married for twenty-two years to, well, it would be unkind to describe the father of my children as a ne'er-do-well. When I still loved him, I just thought of him as a free spirit. You can take your pick. But the bottom line was that I supported the family and he contributed, when or if he could. It was okay during the early years, but two kids added to the burden. He was fine not making the money, but he wasn't especially interested in being a househusband. So it all fell on me. The marriage eventually caved, I escaped with my kids, and I'm dating again. Only this time I'm trying it the other way around. I'd like to know what it feels like to have a man pay for me. So far, it feels . . . weird."

Julie's coach is her former college roommate, an Aspen resident whose own post-marriage history of serial monogamy includes several long-term relationships with men who have supported her financially to one degree or another, simply as a matter of course. The roommate found the idea of picking up a check for a man as alien as cross-dressing. She was happy to tutor Julie, whose marriage struck the roommate as financial abuse, no matter how much feminist thinking both had explored in college.

"When the check comes," the roommate instructed, "you just sit there. It has nothing to do with you. It's his business, because . . . he's the man."

"But it makes me anxious to sit there," Julie explained. "I feel like I should make some gesture."

"Then get up when the check comes and go to the ladies' room. He'll have it handled by the time you get back."

"Yeah, well, what if when I come back he tells me my share?"

"You smile, pay your share, and cross him off the list. You already married one of those. You don't need another round."

These days Julie gives mixed reviews to the philosophy of letting a man pay. "It's a nice feeling to have someone take me to dinner. I get a sense of being, I don't know, valued, even if it's only the price of roast chicken. But I do see a downside. When a man picks up the check, he decides where we go and what we do, because, after all, I'm his guest. I miss that feeling that I'm entitled to my own choices and in my marriage, I made most of them. Maybe I've come too far to stop paying my way. I'm a grown-up and I want to remain one."

Her roommate, naturally, disagrees. "Sure, when you are first dating, he pays and he makes the plans and you might end up eating too much roast beef and not enough sushi, or something of the sort. But once you work out a relationship, the way you spend your time is compromise and negotiation, trying to satisfy both of you. The fact that he picks up the check doesn't have to affect that."

Those are two points of view to test, if you yourself are in the market for a change of expectation. There's a third too, which is a frequent dilemma for women returning to the game. What if you are the one with the financial wherewithal? Would you, as Julie did, pay for a man?

You're more likely to have this option at this point in life than when you were dating in your earlier days. If, for example, you are widowed, you might have been left in comfortable financial circumstances, with most of your financial obligations to educate kids or pay off a mortgage long met. Now you could, if you choose, spend some of your disposable money on travel with an attractive man who unfortunately can't afford his share. Would you?

A divorcée with generous alimony (they are by far in the minority, I know, but some few might be reading at this moment), a woman who has come into a family inheritance, a woman who has achieved a significant level of monetary success in business—women who, for whatever reason, are financially established—might face this dilemma.

In fact, you don't have to have much financial security at all to confront the problem of dating a man who has less than you do. Perfectly nice men are wiped out financially by divorce, hardworking men go bankrupt, businesses fail, careers falter, and plenty of the men you meet just never did that well in the first place (which, you suspect, could be why they are available now). Whatever the reason, you might decide to change your thinking for the sake of companionship. Or, then again, you might not.

"*Don't be a nurse or a purse*—that's the motto of my bereavement group," one woman said. It's a fine motto, but it must be admitted that no one in that group is dating.

"I'm sensitive to my boyfriend's financial situation," said another. "I'm working and he's retired. So we pretty much split things, but we do it in a nice way. Like, he'll pay if we're with his family, but I make sure I pay for dinner the night before. Maybe in the end I end up paying more, because I have more, but I feel like he's careful to put in as much as he can, so I don't feel taken advantage of."

A third offered her solution. "I divorced a very rich guy. A controlling rich guy, although maybe that's saying the same thing. I walked away with a lump sum, just so I wouldn't have to deal with him anymore. My next relationship is with his personality opposite. He is a handsome, sensitive, emotionally attuned artist who owns two shirts and that's about it. I sure didn't want to live his life, stay in his hotels, eat at his restaurants, and no way he could begin to afford mine. So it was either give up my beautiful, sensitive lover or foot the bill. It took me a year of therapy and we were off-again, on-again until I could get clear on my priorities and desires. Now I not only feel okay, frankly, I like getting my way. I see what was in it for my husband all those years. First I divorced him. Now, in a way, I am him. But nicer."

You may not have those financial options, or you might be struggling with the same questions on a smaller scale. What will you pay for, what will he pay for, and what does it mean if you do? Once you've moved to these questions, and especially once they are open questions, discussed and agreed or disagreed upon, you have moved past conversation, sex, and money. You've hit that thing you may have longed for or sworn you'd never try again: You are having a relationship.

CHAPTER EIGHT

Sexual Mentors, Palate Cleansers, and Other Transitional Relationships

It was a gorgeous night, followed by a better morning. Dinner the night before at a glam restaurant with his friends, even holding hands, and she felt she could finally relax into the warmth of his affection. Then the leisurely start of the next day. When they were finally getting up to dress, he reached over to cup her chin. "I'm telling you this because I know you care," he said. "You're starting to put on weight."

Boyfriends

When you resume romantic life with an open heart, you will eventually find yourself in some kind of relationship. With a guy. Who has sorta become, probably temporarily, and for want of a better word, your boyfriend.

Boyfriend—an awkward teenage construct characterizing a

relationship that has some social reliability, an (unspoken, imagined, implied, or openly stated) agreement of sexual exclusivity, but little else defined about it. Whatever role he ends up playing in your life, this relationship has something to teach you. Because, bottom line—boyfriends are not husbands. And that takes some getting used to.

In some respects, boyfriends are a considerable improvement over husbands. For one thing, there is nearly always more sexual frisson, and frankly the more juice a man generates, the better, particularly if you are post-menopausal. Too, boyfriends, especially new ones, try harder to impress you. They recognize that Valentine's Day is a chance to shine. They will bother to talk to your brother because there is no history of mean-spirited competition between them. They often remember to compliment you and frequently clean their own bathrooms. Plus, you can get a few days away from a boyfriend without a fight or the excuse of a business trip because, he is, after all, just a boyfriend. Your time together is circumscribed.

Still, if you had a husband for some time, it's an adjustment to relate to a boyfriend. For starters, what's his is his, in terms of time, money, and general life support. It's his to share if he's generous, or to withhold when he sees fit. Certainly husbands set boundaries too, but so much merges into one blob of *ours* during the years together—our marriage, our children, our luggage, our lawn that needs tending, our gas bill, our books. Our money—especially. It may be that you will never have that kind of *our* again.

You may not want to. Learning as you have from long experience about the difficulties of fair sharing, one or both of you may not be eager to cede control over what you've amassed during the course of a lifetime. So be it. Still, a boyfriend's arbitrary boundaries might require a mental adjustment.

You might want to adjust your own relationship limits too, now that you have the opportunity for a do-over. Do you throw in a boyfriend's underwear as long as you're doing the wash and he's spending three nights a week at your place? Do you think about his dinner if you are out with friends for the evening? Contribute some money if his business deal is teetering? Comment if he sits while you are vacuuming? Or ignore any issue because, after all, he's not going to be around long enough for it to matter?

Think of first boyfriends as a kind of Stage Two of your return to romantic life. Stage One involved all the icebreaking firsts we've discussed in the last several chapters—from your first e-mail exchanges and quick drinks through to your first sexual encounter, if you chose to get that involved. Stage Two is the next toe in the water. All right, it's probably your whole body in the water. In Stage Two you move into some kind of ongoing relationship, for however long it lasts, in whatever form it takes.

You'll likely do a lot of thinking about relationships right around this time. You might even identify with Isabella, a shrewd, exuberant health club owner, who tends to analyze her own romances out of existence. "I think, because I'm older, my relationships are too calculated. I'm trying so hard to make the right decision this time around," she said. "Is this the right man? Will the relationship be fair? Is this a person I could live with? Will he change? Who will he be in ten years? What is his financial situation? Can I have my own space? Will he be too controlling?

"When I fell in love with my husband in my twenties, I didn't think like this at all. I just fell in love. So it was much easier. I've had a series of six- or seven-month relationships—all fix-ups. The men pursue me and it falls into a relationship right away, but after six or seven months I leave, or they do. Because of the thinking I just described."

Men also think hard about what they want, devising guidelines to keep themselves from crashing blind into the mistakes that wrecked the lives of friends. One midsixties divorced pharmacy exec described his own evolving plan:

"The marriage was over for a long time before we separated, and that gave me time to think about how I wanted to handle things. I got married at thirty-three and had lived a pretty promiscuous bachelor's life before my marriage. That ruined a good relationship back then, and I didn't want to go back to that earlier pattern.

"But as soon as word got out that I was separated, I got a ton of phone calls recommending women. Pretty soon I was dating all the time and sleeping with several. These women were all at home, with older kids, and they were all hot to find a relationship. So one thing I got very clear about was that I did not want anyone much younger than me, or anyone with kids at home. I've raised my own kids, I'm very close to them, and I don't want to be involved with child rearing again. I didn't want to be one of those guys who starts a whole new life.

"It took me a good year to learn that about myself, but when I did, it totally straightened out my dating pattern. The women I was meeting didn't *do* anything—except live off their alimony, take care of their kids, go to the gym, talk to their girlfriends. I could quickly see that I would become the center of their lives, way too fast. I remarried last year, to a woman who is more professionally successful than I am, and busier too. I took the time to know what I wanted, and I chose great!"

Other men also reported giving serious thought to their criteria for a second partner. These men tended to be strong managerial types who prided themselves on bringing a balance of rational problem solving and creativity to their business successes. Now circumstances have forced them to bring the same skills to the problems of love. Here is one widowed manufacturing CEO's list of requirements for his next love:

- She must be a peer. I have to like her and feel there is chemistry.
- She must be a loving mother. Does she have a successful relationship with her kids? Does she have some kind of wisdom as a parent?
- She must be a giver. I don't want a taker. I was married to one of those once. Forget it.
- She should know how to communicate and be in a very open, intimate relationship.
- She must be capable of loving me fiercely.

Your own vision of your next relationship will likely change over the course of your dating experiences. The costs of this evolution are in the inevitable false starts and fizzles that can be deadly disappointments to one or both participants. Like the men just quoted, you too will leave some damage in your wake as you try on and discard possible partners.

The common experience of dating someone and then being, for want of a kinder word, dumped, can be excoriating—especially if you are lost in romantic fantasy and therefore unprepared for dating realities. The unexpected loss of another dream, piled onto the loss of a husband or a long-term lover, can be a devastating setback.

Three years later Jeanne reflects on what she feels was the handicap of her double loss. "When my husband didn't want to be married anymore, an old friend stepped into my life to help me through the hard times. I thought, at the time, that he was the Prince, that we were meant to be together, that his presence gave my husband's leaving some kind of positive meaning. I thought this friend and I would live happily ever after. I really, actually believed that. But he didn't stay—so I had a double broken heart."

Construing a transitional relationship as a life partner is such a common distortion that you might almost think of it as the temporary price of doing business. A second woman describes her experience: "I was widowed at fifty-six, and it seemed only normal to me to want to be with a man. I didn't necessarily want to be married, but I didn't want to be alone. I forced myself out into the world—folk dancing, sailing club, synagogue classes. Sometimes I would cry coming home, thinking, 'Why do I have to be here? This is not me!' But I kept on.

"Finally I went to a singles dance—which are awful, by the way, very strained. Someone asked me to dance and we spent a year together. It was strictly physical. I was attracted to him and he helped me have the confidence to have a relationship again. After all, I was twenty-three when I met my husband, and he was the only man I'd ever known. I needed that shot of confidence.

"But I tried to turn the whole thing into a deeper relationship and that didn't work. I wanted to incorporate him into my family, and he just didn't fit. Many times I wanted to do things as a couple and he wasn't available. I guess I had been married so long that I just couldn't see this for the limited sexual fling that it was. We broke up when he didn't show for my birthday party. But you know, even though I knew it wasn't right, I felt very rejected. It was extremely painful—but eventually it got less so. And I was left with a residual confidence that a man who was not my husband could be interested in me.

"I have to say, I did this two more times—had two more flings that broke up when I tried to bring the man into my life. Both times when we broke up I was just devastated. But I think I needed these three experiences to understand myself. I want a man *in* my life, not on the edges. About five years ago I met a widower who wanted a life with me. Now he *is* my family."

That resilient widow kept going after three disappointing experiences, but not everyone has the same emotional energy. One thrice-divorced grandmother has lately withdrawn from romantic life because two bad dating experiences have shaken her. "Both men had closer involvements with other women than they initially led me to believe. One situation ended with the other woman harassing me. The other required a restraining order when my boyfriend couldn't cope with my breaking up with him. Since then I've taken myself out of the market—no clubs, organizations, no church socials, no groups of people my own age at all. I think I'm protecting myself. I'm extremely happy with my life situation right now in terms of being close to my family and enjoying my job. I keep thinking, 'Look at all you have. Don't mess it up with man problems.'"

Her experience is not uncommon. It is, after all, a long life, and you're meeting men who have lived plenty of it. Naturally they have baggage. Unfortunately, you are likely to trip over it, especially if you don't proceed slowly and carefully.

"I was frankly elated with my divorce, but a year later I had my first heartbreak. I had a passionate first date that went on for a month. I instantly started including this man in my life, meeting my elderly parents, the whole nine yards. Then he revealed a three-year relationship with a married woman that he was not willing to give up. He and I cross paths now, but I have become an expert at being in the same room and not seeing him."

Men do acknowledge the hard limits of their involvement, though not necessarily to you, and not necessarily at first. "My relationships all begin with chemistry and crash on the rocks of compatibility," said a retired pilot whose daughter is his longest sustained companion. "I like to fall asleep to the TV, and when a woman moves in—it's happened twice in the last ten years—she wants the TV off. Or she wants the couch on a different wall. Or she wants some change made for her, something. I am perfectly happy as I am. We start to fight and pretty soon I am starting over with another woman."

Or this confession, from an attorney who has been single for five years: "How do I end a relationship when I don't want to go further? I'm not proud to say it, but I do what most men do: I disappear."

Don't allow yourself to relax comfortably into the Men Bad/ Women Good stance. While it allows for highly satisfactory venting, it totally skews your social analysis. It is true that men flee relationships. That is, some men flee all committed relationships, and all men dodge some of them, at some time. You're right about that.

But the fact is, women flee committed relationships too. Some women dodge all of them, and most women evade some of them, some of the time. We don't necessarily disappear, though that has been known to happen. But we do cut the cord, walk away, and hurt men in the process.

We leave for the same reasons that men do—because the glow has faded, we met someone better, or we got close enough to see something ugly, at least in our eyes. One physician's assistant said, "The first guy I started seeing took me to great places and that was a fresh treat for me. Plus, he was fun and made me laugh. But he seemed . . . demanding. One night I was late because I got hung up with my family. When I finally got in the car, he wasn't speaking to me. Sulking. I looked at him and thought, 'Wait a minute—didn't I just go through hell to divorce a demanding sulker?' That was it for me."

Men and women also leave because these transitional relationships are inevitably experienced through the prism of the loss from which you are recovering. It definitely affects your view. A divorced landscape architect reflected on her own emotional reserve after her marriage came apart. "I met a guy through a friend and we hit it off. We had a relationship for five months. I knew right away that he was a good guy, but initially I couldn't even tell you what he looked like. I now hold men at such a distance that I was really slow to take him in—I mean, you know, to actually look at him. I remember seeing him across a table one night and thinking, 'Gee, he's actually cute.'

"He lived out of town and that was fine by me, but I couldn't get comfortable integrating him into my own life. I would visit him, but I never wanted him to come here. I'm cautious by nature, and when he wanted to move the relationship forward, I was done."

Other women, decidedly single, deliberately seek a temporary boyfriend—whether because they are afraid to hope for more, or because they have firmly determined to put up with less. "I'm not looking for someone to walk through a hundred years with," says one divorced filmmaker now in her sixties. "I'm just there for a little while, to enjoy what there is about this particular guy. When we stop making memories together, when he doesn't have time for me or other priorities seem to invade his life, I don't try to fix things. I just give him a hug and send him on his way. New adventures come along every day, for as long as they last."

Even if you believe you are seeking a longer-lasting partnership, you might still be so affected by the one you've lost that you punish the person with whom you wake up. "Shortly after my divorce," said the stay-at-home ex-wife of a developer, "I met a really, well, nice guy, the kind of guy who, if he wanted a date and I had the kids, would say, 'Well, bring them along.' I realized later that I was incredibly difficult with him. I did not show him my loving, trusting side at all. I had been very wounded by my marriage and I was so self-protective then. He wanted me and I was always deciding that he wasn't good enough or he wasn't the right one and then I'd break up with him. Pretty soon I'd get lonely and we'd get back together and I'd start up doing the same thing again.

"It was the opposite of my distant husband, where I was the adoring one and eventually my husband decided that I wasn't good enough, so he left. By the time I realized the dynamic and how I was destroying this new relationship, the damage I had done was irreparable. We went into couples therapy, but we just couldn't get past the fact that I had dumped him three times. Eventually he withdrew and it was too late to get him back."

Can't get him back, can't let him go. Can't commit to

moving forward yourself, can't get him to return a phone call. Can't live without him or can't remember what you could possibly have been thinking. Can't stop crying, can't feel a thing. Prepare yourself for the temporary roller coaster of emotional regression.

Transitional Setbacks

Progress is not always made in forward motion. It might involve a sidestep, even a backward glance. Especially when we measure an emotional or spiritual passage, it's clear that a kind of doubling back occurs. We re-create old themes, confront old issues, finally stare down old demons. It's the looking back in a fresh way that allows for some kind of move ahead. But be prepared. A step back frequently takes us into old emotional pain. That regression can come as an unpleasant surprise.

Surely you carry with you the memory of the girl you were in your single years. True, she might have been more playful, happy, and free. But like many women, your younger version was probably also less mature—more anxious, fretful, suspicious, guarded, or wildly emotional—than the woman into whom you've morphed.

Perhaps you drank more in those days, dramatized more, called your girlfriends no matter what time, and wept more than the woman you eventually became. Maybe you were just much less confident, less able to start a conversation, walk alone into a party, make a decision, or insist on getting proper credit or a fair raise. You might even have been symptomatic in those days, pulling your hair, binging or purging, or given to long, bleak, socially isolated periods of despair. Or maybe you just used lots of bad judgment, secondary to loneliness, inexperience, and wishful thinking.

Whatever were your personal weak spots, over time things probably evened out. Somewhere during the course of your marriage you may have even taken the time to pat yourself on the back for the inner distance you'd traveled. You may or may not have been struggling in the harbor of your relationship, but you were no longer so much at sea with your personal demons.

And now they're back.

It's a helluva thing to find yourself weeping in your foyer over a man who did not kiss you good night, only now you are a grandmother. It's a nightmare to feel those old uncertain, paranoid thoughts creep in—"*What's he after? Don't believe a word*"—when you've only been invited over for dinner. Or to hear yourself—previous classroom mom, committee chair, happy organizer you—making transparent excuses to dodge a cocktail party when the real reason is that you fear no one will talk to you.

These days you could find yourself spending way too much time drinking or crying, staring dully at Lifetime movies or ranting to your cat. You hang up after a perfectly fine conversation with a man and down a pint of Häagen-Dazs. You have four dates with a decent orthodontist and suddenly you are sitting in desperate hope by the phone. You are back to picking your cuticles or, much worse, back to smoking. You are back, it seems, to the girl you'd outgrown. What's wrong with you?

You're dating. It sets us back for a while.

Sure it could be something much worse, much more serious. Certainly if you've gone to any extreme, or if your emotional regression lasts for over a year or it's doing serious damage, you'd be wise to get professional help. That should get you back up to emotional speed. But chances are great that your regression, albeit unpleasant and unnerving, is all too normal.

Many women report this common experience of emotional regression when they begin to date. It's as if earlier psychological issues are like a deep underground river that, surprisingly, is still flowing. But you can get yourself up and out. In fact, that's one of the tasks of this transitional time.

Emotional regression only means that your earlier, less mature emotional responses and self-destructive patterns—ones you've long since developed beyond—have reemerged during this stressful time. Where you thought you'd become more stable and secure, it appears that you'd only become safely married. Now, turned single without even the illusion of being loved, you are scared and set back.

Although this setback is often temporary (meaning months, but not years), it feels so . . . teenage, that it can be really troubling. For one thing, emotional pain is real—it's visceral and it hurts. It's a heaviness in your heart, a racing, restless discomfort inside your own skin, a choking throat or some dull, constant muscle ache. You feel bad and you say so, but without much relief. Your still-safely-married friends start to look askance and wonder if you really are okay. And you start to wonder yourself.

Chances are, you are fine. Dating is essentially a late-adolescent activity, and it returns you momentarily to your late-adolescent self. Besides, emotional regression under new stress is to be expected. If you can clearly identify yours, that will be a step toward finding your way back to adulthood. Certainly you will have your own unique version of emotional setbacks. But here are some of the common issues, which might help you spot your own:

- Separation pain.
- Trust issues.
- Fear of rejection.
- Destructive relationship patterns.

Separation pain is that bleak agitated grief that overcomes some of us when we must part from a person to whom we are attached. The homesickness you felt at summer camp is a common and very understandable form of this emotional pain, as is the mini depression you fell into when a close friend moved away.

Some people experience a more acute variety of this pang— tearful at every good-bye, even if it's a fifth date; flung into a few hours or days of hard sadness when a lover takes a trip or sometimes even when he takes a night off. You *know* the separation from you is normal, needed, reasonable, even impersonal. But you *feel* the pain anyway. That's separation pain.

For years on end, a solid, committed marriage can act as the antidote to your propensity toward separation pain. Your sense of love's continuity, even in the temporary absence of your partner, can totally erase the anxious, irrational stab of loss you suffered in your younger, lonelier days. You had, in fact, thought you'd outgrown your separation pangs, if you thought about it at all. Then your mate dies, or you divorce, and suddenly your old anguish revisits you.

The ending of a date makes you suffer, and sometimes you keep a man in bed with you just to avoid the bad feeling of saying good night. Take a weekend trip with a new boyfriend and the Sunday night of your return to separate quarters can be a tough one to get through on your own. You might cling to your kids more than is good for them, just to ward off your own internal ache.

Managing separation pain has its risks too. Certainly any small reconnection temporarily takes the edge off, which is why his brief phone call or the establishment of a next date magically makes you sane and relaxed again. But you can't force that phone call or those future plans, so it's easy for that old longing to get out of hand.

You may have learned to keep your own angst under control. You call your girlfriends to analyze his behavior, or sometimes just to mention his name. You make some small, harmless effort to reconnect—find a pretext to call or send a friendly e-mail, get one in response, and feel just fine.

Some vulnerable few, though, feel such agony in the uncertainty of dating that they are unable to tolerate the period of silence between dates. They call frequently, drop off small cards and gifts, even drive by someone's home so as to make contact if only symbolically. Like any other ill considered pain medication, these brief reconnections can be short acting and have side effects. You end up looking needy, becoming intrusive, and so actually push away the object of your interest.

Separation pain can also stir whatever past impulse you've had to self-medicate, whether through food or drugs or alcohol or television or all of the above. If you have any of these signs, you've likely regressed back to your old lonely heartache.

Past **trust issues** that resurface can be similarly destructive, though they are more likely to turn their poison outward, sabotaging new relationships. Looking back, you recognize that it was always hard for you to trust men, that you were naturally guarded and possibly also injured by some early experiences with deceit. Maybe your dad betrayed your mom and taught by example what you should watch out for. Or maybe you just sensed that he could.

Either way, early boyfriends were always suspect, and often you were proved right. We have an uncanny way of attracting what we fear, so you may well have had enough experiences with untrustworthy men to make your own issues seem entirely theirs. Your marriage may have lulled these suspicions, or, depending upon the integrity of your husband, exacerbated them.

Dating again brings your old trust issues to the fore. Your emotional regression shows itself in the new stiff distance you keep and the defensive way you interact. You don't emotionally connect easily or well. You test often, making unreasonable demands or setting cold, hard boundaries and expecting a new partner to tolerate your fences. You give a new guy a hard time, or no time at all. You have unwittingly built a defensive castle with the unconscious expectation that someone worthy will swim the moat and brave your slings and arrows to prove himself. Some may try; others walk away. It sure gets lonely waiting.

The **fear of rejection** reintroduces you to your old, self-critical scaredy-cat. That internal voice is so absorbed in a monologue of your fears and flaws that she can't risk exposure to new people. Chapter 4 cataloged the *too old, too fat, too tired* mantra to which you might find yourself especially susceptible these days. You'll add to it your own old pet fear, the one that may have dimmed to a whisper during your long relationship years and is now screaming again in your head: You're too boring, too slow, too ill informed or unattractive to attract any interest. Why bother?

Fear of rejection, with its paralyzing thoughts and stomach-clenching dread, sends you to the sidelines because that's the only safe place to be. Between romantic life itself and the sidelines where you've stashed yourself looms a psychological barrier that appears insurmountable—at least while you are in this state of emotional regression.

Actually, that barrier is only tissue-thin. A social risk—a party entered solo, a dinner alone, the movies by yourself, and then an invitation extended to a new friend, a tour on which you embark without knowing a soul, a smile at a strange man, a party you host where you invite a crush or even two—and then the next risk and the next. Some will be met with rejection, some with applause. But you will have found your way back into life and possibly back into romance as well.

Finally, a common emotional regression is the detour we make back into some **old unworkable relationship patterns with men**. It's as if dating itself is a Magna Doodle, instantly erasing our emotional progress and sending us back to the old destructive needs and fantasies of our youth. If you had a distinctive dysfunctional dating pattern that you finally overcame, you might engage in a transitional relationship that touches base briefly with the confused girl you were. Then you can finally shed that old skin and resume romantic life as the woman you've become. Hopefully.

For example, if you always dated players but finally married a good guy, you might find yourself in a go-round or two with your old handsome heartbreaker type before you catch on to yourself. If you used to put up with boyfriends who were fine partners but lousy lovers, you might re-create another round of that old frustrating compromise.

If you were drawn to married alpha males and staged painful losing competitions with their long-suffering wives, you will be especially vulnerable to the married men who can sniff out your attraction. If you had a weakness for arty, self-absorbed losers, well, you're apt to break your heart over an underdeveloped musician or two before you get back on your feet. Or you might have a self-destructive pattern all your own to revisit and then lay to rest.

Sometimes, ironically enough, the pattern that didn't work well earlier turns out to be just fine at this point in life. One recently divorced woman described her own appreciation of a newly liberated agenda this way: "My old pattern was to have brief, wacky, maniacal interludes with some man who was totally out of my main frame—wrong social class or educational level, someone who only connects with some small part of me. He'd be someone I'd meet, say, when I was hiking, or doing some kind or retreat. He's usually sweet and calm and unambitious and would never fit into my social world.

"The only man I ever dated who did fit my social picture—financially, socially, intellectually—was the man I married and had my kids with. Once we were divorced, though, and I was through having kids, I thought I'd earned the right to enjoy exactly the kind of man I was always drawn to, but knew enough not to marry. And that's what I'm doing now. It's my version of happily ever after."

Your own early romantic pattern may no longer present a

problem either. Most likely, though, if it didn't work then, it won't work now, and you'll want to catch yourself in the act and extricate yourself.

But how? There's no quick cure for emotional regression, of whatever variety. In the case of a destructive relationship pattern, you'll want to identify it as soon as possible, steel yourself, and stop it cold in its tracks.

Fear of rejection recedes in the face of brave action, however small and steady.

Trust issues require a fair amount of self-talk to persuade you that it's safe to let down your guard. A new, tested, and trustworthy man can only go so far to rebuild your trust. You will have to take yourself the rest of the way.

And separation pain must be labeled and endured until it passes. Friends help, reading helps, exercise helps, and a good night's sleep does too. So does reminding yourself, over and over, that you've felt this before, and, however acute, emotional pain passes. Then do all these things that you've learned—through your divorce or widowhood, or just over the course of life—will make your own emotional pain pass more easily.

In every one of these examples of emotional regression, or in your own variety, the key is to be on to yourself. When you can clearly label your emotional reactions as the setbacks they are, you will be apt to get through them more quickly. Your adult, rational, and even more mature self is still in there. She's just emotionally overwhelmed by old stuff. Keep steering forward and you'll find her again—farther along than you had remembered.

Those setbacks, and the progress you've made in overcoming them, are unlikely to occur in isolation. Many times they occur in a kind of tandem with a certain kind of boyfriend—in the predictable, if temporary partnership of the transitional relationship.

Transitional Relationships

In the end, boyfriends, especially boyfriends early in your post-long-relationship experience, are more than flirtations or flings. They are projection screens, whipping boys, tutors, lifesavers, belt notches, social covers, and healing balms. Although each relationship has its distinctive story, there is a pattern to these transitional romances. They usually come in one of four flavors:

- The palate cleanser.
- The functional guy.
- The caretaker.
- The sexual mentor.

Your boyfriend might fit into more than one of the above. Generally speaking, though, transitional romances fall into one of these categories.

The Palate Cleanser: Mr. Antithesis

This transitional relationship is a billboard for some significant element that was missing in the relationship you left behind.

You can't always read the signs, of course. Sometimes you are standing just too close. Ask yourself, though, "In what way does this new boyfriend seem very different from my last relationship?" Then consider the possibility that it is this very difference that drew you to him in the first place.

The palate cleanser is that transitional man who is the opposite of your last relationship in some crucial way, and thus makes your changeover from that relationship easier. He's a taste break, someone who clears your heart and mind and holds open the possibility of new experiences. The specific need that was unfulfilled in your last relationship is an itch that has long gone unscratched. It's common for you to head straight for that scratching post and, at least for a while, revel in the new satisfaction you feel.

It might be a trait you've found in your new lover that was definitely absent from your husband. Your palate cleanser is mechanical, organized, and competent where your ex was intellectual and generally inept. You feel taken care of in a whole different way. Or he's socially connected, a people person, and you are enjoying a social life unavailable to you during your marriage to a more introspective homebody.

Alternatively, this new boyfriend might be blessedly free of some toxic part of your past lover's personality. For example, twenty years of marriage to a verbal slasher leaves your shoulders wedged up around your ears. This new lover's even calm acts as a spa treatment for your leftover anxiety. Or your palate cleanser might be the direct, take-charge man who erases the taste of a passive-aggressive husband, or he might be Mr. Distance, who gives you room to breathe after a long marriage to Mr. Control Freak.

Those differences might show themselves in small, telling ways. One ex-wife observed, "I was married to a man who collected watches—beautiful, expensive, fancy watches. The man

I date now doesn't even own a watch. That pretty much says it all."

Or some altered aspect of life circumstances—neighborhood, income, the presence or absence of children—could make this transitional boyfriend satisfying in a way that your lost love could not be. For example, to be with a young, vigorous man after the two years you spent caring for your failing, older spouse might be so magnetically appealing that it's months before you realize there is nothing to talk about. Or your palate cleanser might be a man who is eager to get married, the ideal antidote to your eleven years with the commitment-phobic boyfriend.

Sometimes your own financial circumstances have shifted, and with that the whole power balance of your relationships with men. One divorced woman, who was dumped by a wealthy, guilty husband, came away with a damaged spirit and a large-enough share of the joint assets to give her financial independence. The combination made her view her first serious boyfriend from a skeptical distance for years. "I chose him because he made me feel so good. He adored me, doted on me, gave me all the emotional support that my husband withheld. But I had a voice in my head that said, 'You're on the rebound. Don't get hooked up. Maybe he just wants the money.' I don't support him, but I do contribute a lot to the kitty. It took me years before I could trust that."

The palate cleanser satisfies acute emotional needs that remain after a long famine. Antithesis relationships will certainly have issues of their own (what relationship doesn't?), but those issues might take a while to surface. Initially you can be so soothed by the fresh taste that it's easy to get in deeper than the relationship merits. Palate cleansers therefore come with a high risk of premature commitment on your part.

Sometimes the attraction is obvious and the risk is minimal. One newly divorced high school coach took his sons on a sailing trip and began a nice conversation with a woman who ran an art gallery at the marina. He followed up with an e-mail, and pretty soon he was traveling out of town every other weekend to see her. "It was a lot of driving," he said, "but the draw was simple. She was so affectionate with me. My wife hadn't wanted much to do with me for the last several years. This woman really liked me and seemed so happy to have me around. That made it a lot of fun." The relationship ended with a bang, though, after about a year. "She wanted more, wanted to start being included on the weekends when I had my sons. I didn't think they were ready for that—and I guess I wasn't either. That was that. But in the time I spent with her, you know, she helped me put myself back together again."

A second man reflected on his palate cleansers as reentry relationships, more matters of convenience than affairs of the heart, but definitely meeting a need that his last serious girlfriend was unable to. "After my last bad breakup, I dated two women in a row, both of whom took me back to the social world I had enjoyed when I was younger. Early on, the first woman invited me to a family holiday dinner, and I was immediately able to connect with her family in a way that I had never been able to with my long-term girlfriend. This new family were just more my kind of people, and I felt so much more at ease. The next woman was actually someone I had had a crush on when I was fourteen. I loved being back in the world where I saw old friends.

It was just a visit, though. It wasn't reason enough to make those relationships last."

Still, sometimes the very antithesis of the experience hooks you in some deep place, then leaves you in a wrenching dilemma. That can happen to a man or woman.

Lizanne walked out on her successful, rigid, and workaholic husband of thirty years when she fell in love. Her lover was an aspiring opera singer/bartender with whom she shared a passion for poetry, theater, and sex. "All those years I begged my husband to just take a walk on the beach with me, but he hated to be away from his work. All those times when I would cry and carry on and fight with my husband and he would just look at me like I had lost my mind and leave the room till I calmed down. To meet a man who talks, actually talks about his feelings, about me, about us. A man who loved to be with me, kiss me. A man who focused all his attention and passion toward me. Well . . . it was irresistible. I was able to move forward with a divorce, and I'm so glad I made that life change. I never would have done it, I don't think, if I hadn't gotten a taste of what I had been missing all those years. I mean, I knew what I was missing—but knowing it and feeling it are two different things."

Lizanne continued, "My affair lasted two more sweet, wrenching, passionate, crazed years. Finally my lover went back to his own wife, the woman who had mothered him and sheltered him and grounded him so he could be the crazy, unfocused emotional opera singer that he is. The end about killed me, even though I knew by then that we couldn't make a life together, because he was way too much of a kid for me, even though he was fifty-two. Still, I found what I was missing. Maybe too big a dose of it, but I'm not going to do without it again.

"By the way," she added, "my husband replaced me within four months, with a perfectly pleasant auditor who wears theme sweaters on holidays and never appears to get excited about anything. It definitely worked out all around." In some cases, apparently, palate cleansers are long-term soothers.

And sometimes they are short-term solutions. An intense sexual connection is a common palate-cleansing experience, if only because in long-term relationships the sexual energy flickers dim, whereas we are drawn to new partners in large part because of the sexual interest they kindle. For a while, sexual desire stirs us to imagine more than what might be there.

"When I divorced my dullard of a husband—why did I waste twenty-one years there?—I'll tell you, I had an affair with my married squash partner. He left his wife and moved in with me and pretty much stepped into the spot left by my ex. My kids were out of the house by then, but they were happy to see me happy. I was living my same life but with great sex, and that was what I was looking for. In the end, though, when I got to know him, I discovered that the problem was he was all about sex—watching porn, sending dirty e-mails to his ex-wives, basically, if not cheating on me, then certainly having a sneaky private life. I couldn't trust that, so we ended. You'll think I got what I deserve, but it got me past my divorce and back into bed, so I healed pretty fast."

The sexual need you are filling might be so satisfying that the agony of its complications is worth the price—for a while. One widow described her affair with a married man with painfully mixed feelings. "Mark and I fulfilled each other's needs of the moment. I needed to be appreciated and I needed sex. I'm very physical. He had a wife with whom he doesn't have sex, so we fit perfectly together. I thought he'd be . . . a placeholder. He's not the relationship I'm looking for. But it's been three years, and when I see something interesting, he's the person I call."

Men too try palate cleansers and find they sometimes become a central emotional focus. One lifelong married widower described the quicksand in which he found himself, caught in a fervent lasting embrace with a woman who did not fit into his world. She did, however, fit into his bed and into his imagination. Perfectly.

He explained that his beloved wife was a perfect partner, wife, and mother. She was petite, conservative, and a community role model. Her loss to lung cancer was traumatic for the whole family. Six months later, after only two dates, he found himself naked in the arms of a tall, cleavage-flaunting, way-too-young bombshell whose idea of culture was Neiman Marcus.

"I was only having fun," he says. "But it's been four years and I'm still in it. I don't want to be without her; don't want to sleep without her. But not a single person I know—not friends, not family—no one is comfortable around her. I don't blame my friends. She doesn't make an effort to get to know them. She just shows up waving her . . . her . . . okay, her breasts. She'll sit and lean them into me and just look at me and not talk to my friends. The women hate her and the men don't know where to look. I know she's rude because she's just nervous around my world, but I can't imagine making a life with her. It's caused a wedge between my family and me, and I don't want that. So we keep breaking up. But I sneak and see her and don't tell anyone. And I'm sixty-three years old. It's ridiculous."

Ridiculous or not, a palate cleanser can bring such powerful emotional, sexual, or spiritual satisfaction that many other needs will be sacrificed on that altar. Such a sacrifice might be all to your good if you discover that your palate needed cleansing of all those social expectations you've tried so hard to satisfy. Getting naked at this time of life may allow you to look beyond pleasing others to identify your own unique preferences.

You might even consciously decide to suit yourself at this point in life—the opinions of others be damned. As one widow explained of her younger and far less successful lover, "The husband was someone I chose for building a life with. My lover is for me."

The Functional Relationship and the Caretaker

These two transitional relationships step in to fill recently emptied shoes. Your needs might be so acute, though, that for a while you confuse function with feeling.

As we discussed earlier, turning single can be an isolating experience in a largely couples world. A purely functional relationship at least eases your social transition—until (if and when) you are ready for a more meaningful connection. Many people newly returned to the game deliberately seek out just such a transitional person, often in the form of a return to ex-lovers who have evolved into old friends.

New acquaintances can serve this transitional function too. One man, recently separated from his third wife, described his choices straightforwardly. "I don't care to socialize alone. It's awkward. But I'm much more cautious at this point about getting sexually or emotionally involved. I go very slow now and let it go with a kiss good night for a long time. Still, I want to have the company of a date.

"With this separation, early on I went to a party and met a sophisticated, good-looking woman who had proper manners and two nice daughters. When I had something to go to, a party or a charity event, she made a very pleasant date. But there was no intimacy—not sexually or emotionally. So pretty soon I lost interest and just stopped calling her. There's always a new woman to fill that role."

Others, male and female, come to appreciate the emotionally protected preserve their functional friendships afford. Sixty-eight-year-old Denise lives a fair drive from Bill, a vigorous seventy-four. Theirs is a solid, seven-year, platonic, and highly functional relationship, which each expects to last until death does them part.

Denise explained her attitude. "I knew Bill from years ago, before we were both married. We got together after his divorce. It's not a sexual relationship, which is great, because there is no pressure for anything. We just have a good time together. I see him every weekend, though not necessarily every night of the weekend. He has a theater subscription, we go to concerts, we like so many of the same things. But we don't try to make it more than that. We had dated so many years ago and hadn't had romantic feelings for each other, so it was easy to reestablish this purely platonic connection."

But what about the possibility of romance in her own life over all these years? "Well," she said, "I had a very, very bad marriage, and I think I was damaged. I couldn't dream of taking that kind of risk again. Then too, neither of us wants to give up our independence. We just enjoy being able to get up and go without having to answer to anyone. So this arrangement works well for both of us."

Denise and Bill have made a realistic, functional friendship the satisfying center of their emotional lives. But some of us, longing for more, distort those functional connections. Quite often there's a hard bump at the end. One forty-nine-year-old widow described just such an abrupt awakening.

"For two years after my husband died, I socialized but did no dating. I just grieved and focused on working on myself and getting my kids on safe ground. Once they were out of the house, I decided I was ready, so I went to a dating service. The first guy and I exchanged e-mails, met, and had a nine-month relationship. During that time I thought we were totally involved with each other. We met each other's families, mixed lives; I spent time with his kids, the whole deal.

"Then he blew me off one night. Wouldn't tell me what was wrong. Pretty soon he just stopped calling. I was frankly shocked, but on reflection I realized that we spent so much time together, but we weren't close at all. He was so very shut down, never wanted to answer my questions. And I ignored that because I think I was just tired of being alone. I was so used to being with someone in my marriage, I think I just needed a warm body to show up next to me."

There's nothing wrong with a warm body showing up next to you. It's easy to pretend, though, that you have found a warm heart to go along with it. This widow was painfully bruised by her companion's disappearing act; it took her some time to reengage, to trust her instincts, to chance another attachment. Hers was the common risk of the functional relationship: The form is so compelling, it's easy to gull yourself into believing that feeling is behind it. And eventually feeling will out.

Even when there is genuine feeling behind the form, a relationship may still be suitable only for this transition time in your life. This is the case with the transitional caretaker relationship. The person with the genuine feeling is apt to be the caretaker. If you are the one on the receiving end, what you are probably feeling, instead of adult affection, is needy needy needy. Given the painful changes in your life, who could blame you?

A caretaker is a special form of functional relationship. It's a person who steps beyond the social or sexual space left by your partner and directly into a domestic, financial, or parenting partnership with you. All this occurs at a moment in life when you are probably at your most vulnerable. That makes you ripe for dependence, at least until you can once again take care of yourself. By that time, if you're not cautious, you could be in deep.

The caretaker assumes the role your long-term partner vacated. He usually steps in at your invitation ("Do you think I should repair the furnace or just get a new one?" "Do I want term life insurance? Or the other kind?") and often with your deep gratitude, at least at first. He might, for example, take over the tasks once the purview of the husband you've lost or left— supervising your car inspection, confronting the plumber, helping you refinance the mortgage, driving at night.

Not every newly single woman needs this kind of support. Your long-term relationship may have been less gender-biased, or you might have been partnered with an incompetent boob and so learned to do it all yourself. To the degree that you were less dependent on the partner you lost, you are probably less vulnerable to a caretaker than some other woman might be. On the other hand, for sure you are more tired.

Even if you handled all the administrative and maintenance issues of adulthood on your own, new issues come up once you are separated or widowed that you might never have considered.

An involved caretaker might talk to your divorce lawyer on your behalf, then take the time to explain things to you at a slower pace. He might even step in and discipline your twenty-year-old who has started drinking too much—something your son's dad would have done were he not recently AWOL from fatherhood. The caretaker tends to do all this seamlessly, as if you'd been partnering for years instead of for the few months you've known him. You don't merely allow it—you welcome it.

One woman, explaining a disastrous second marriage to her transitional caretaker, said, "When I got dumped and divorced at fifty, I hadn't ever even paid a bill. I didn't know how to keep a damn record of checks. It was just overwhelming. My new boyfriend offered to help me. Actually, seeing me struggle, he got impatient and insisted. I didn't fight it, for sure. One weekend I brought the whole mess over to him in a garbage bag. I fell asleep and when I woke up he had all my paperwork in neat piles on his desk. I took one look at those piles and thought I was in love. I was remarried three months later and pretty soon I realized he would try to organize my whole life into strict little piles. I was stupid and helpless and that's how I got to divorce number two."

A second woman, divorced with twin high school juniors, re-married a caretaking, take-charge boyfriend and noted that her ex-husband remarried a female version of the same personality type. "My ex and I are both artists, very laissez-faire and hope-less with child discipline. I married an engineer the second time around, and my ex married a nursing supervisor. Occasion-ally the four of us meet to talk about reining in the kids—who really do go nuts with friends and money and drinking over their summer vacation. At one meeting I noticed that the two stepparents were going on and on about rules and responsibility and my ex and I had totally stopped participating. We just handed the problem off to our spouses and were going on our dreamy way. I caught my ex's eye and we almost started to laugh, but we stopped ourselves. Afraid we'd get in trouble with the spouses, I guess."

Not all caretakers are control freaks, and not every widow or divorcée is needy—but take-charge men and dependent, newly single women find each other, just as passive or confused single men and hypercompetent, highly responsible women are magnetized to each other when they cross paths.

In the transition, such a pairing only makes sense. Suppose you are dealing with an intimidating attorney or a pushy real estate agent. You need someone with whom to talk it all over. Your friends are interested and supportive, but they have their own lives. Your caretaking boyfriend, however, focuses on you, supports you, and steps in on your behalf. It's more than sublimely satisfying. It's often essential to getting through this hard time.

The thing is, your hard times will end. You will be ready for a more equal relationship, and that will be an adjustment challenge for both you and your caretaker. Very often, caretakers—whether giving, controlling, or a bit of both—turn out to be guys on whom we can depend, but not the ones we necessarily love. That's a painful pill for you both. Mr. Caretaker may not deserve it, but the romance does not always survive the transition.

Women frequently fall into the caretaker role too, supporting newly single men who are having difficulty steering by themselves. Naturally, caretaking women also frequently feel unappreciated, if not utterly shafted, when the newly single male gets back on his emotional feet. That's why women are warned against dating men who are recently divorced or, God forbid, only separated. You are very likely to end up doing what one experienced woman described as "bachelor rehab."

Bachelor rehab refers to the loving support that a single woman, maybe even one divorced or widowed herself, offers to a recently single man with whom she becomes involved. Just like most women coming out of a relationship, this divorcing man feels fragile and almost embarrassed. It's strange to be out and about with someone other than his wife. His family has fallen apart, and people close to him—whether his ex, his kids, or his own parents or friends—may blame him for it. He's coping with their anger, his own fury and loss, financial upheaval, and the utter disruption of his daily routine.

It's not a time when he's feeling great about himself, any more than you probably were at that same point in your life. A caretaker relationship is all about making his load lighter and making him feel happier. For sure that will work, especially if you are good at it. But will it work well for you?

Women taking on (whether consciously or unconsciously) the task of bachelor rehab offer support, advice, and comfort to make this man feel good about himself again. They offer a positive sexual experience—which for a man who likely hasn't been enjoying marital sex for some time goes a long way toward making him feel better. These supportive women offer guidance too, sometimes along the same traditional gender lines that males offer. Male caretakers talk lawyers, finances, and water heater maintenance. Female caretakers may offer professional expertise in these areas as well. They will also strategize about the best ways to heal the breach with adult daughters, propose shrewd techniques to set limits with an angry ex-wife, and suggest decorating tips for stripped-down bachelor households.

As with women in transitional, caretaking relationships, new bachelors usually seek out this support and are very grateful to receive it. But again, the caretaking romance can quickly come to resemble an intimate marriage in form, without the necessary feelings to back it up. After the year or so that it takes for a new bachelor to get his single sea legs—that is, to straighten out all the money, to work out the child care or relationships with his adult kids, to set up a new home—bachelor rehab is complete. Like any male caretaker, you could be left behind when your patient has made a full recovery and is ready to set out on his own. Being left behind after all you've given is a particularly galling experience.

Does this mean that all functional relationships fail to progress to love? Not at all. Some initially lackluster social escorts develop into stable life partners. Soul mate or not, some of us marry our caretakers and are forever grateful for their life support. Even palate cleansers can provide such unexpected and heretofore unknown satisfaction that we live happily ever, having made a better compromise in this new relationship than the old one could provide. Relationships, especially romantic ones, take plot turns that even the most experienced of daters or psychologists can only shrug over.

But don't bet on it.

THE SEXUAL MENTOR

This transitional relationship reintroduces you to the physical plea-sures of getting naked again. You might pay a brief emotional price, but the rewards can be terrific.

Here's the thing. Sex is tricky. Before it can be fun, it's anx-ious and uncomfortable. No, not for everyone, not all the time, and not always around the same issues. But for many

—especially with the prospect of facing the judgment of a new partner;

—or if your last long-term sexual partner was your only one, or at least the only one in recent memory;

—or if the only other person who has seen you naked lately is your doctor;

—or if you have some wild idea that your body is imperfect . . . and perhaps especially if your long-term partner came to that same conclusion and turned to some other, more at-tractive body to satisfy himself;

—or if you don't mind the *idea* of sex but your actual experi-ence of desire appears to have died;

—or if you have fixed on some personal inadequacy—your inability to orgasm, the gag reflex you can't control dur-ing oral sex, your thunder thighs, morning gas, undereye circles—any or all of which would be painfully, humiliat-ingly revealed in bed;

—or for any other negative thought unique to your own history well then, getting naked and enjoying sex might be, as noted earlier, anxious and uncomfortable. What then?

When faced with this discomfort, some of us grit our teeth and bulldoze our way through, and that'll certainly work. These women are frank about their anxieties, but determined not to let those fears keep them out of bed. As one announced, "The first time I got to the third date and decided to make it a sexual encounter, I forced myself to leave the lights on. I didn't back into the bathroom either, just turned around naked and kept on walking. It's gotten easier."

Truth be told though, this same woman and several others confessed that they chose icebreaker men, or men in whom they had little emotionally invested, to try out these first revealing naked walks to the bathroom. "I tried it out first with a man I was not remotely interested in having a relationship with," said one widow, describing her first lover after forty years of marriage. "I thought of him as a, well, a test balloon." All giggles aside, the test worked.

In other words, in one form or another, these women found sexual mentors. Maybe you should consider doing the same?

Literature and lore refer to an old, perhaps vaguely European cultural rite of sexual education. The idea was that, at a certain age, a young man would be introduced to sexual pleasures by a worldly older woman who knew the ropes and enjoyed herself in the process. In theory, at least, everyone profits. The young man becomes a more experienced lover, able to provide more physical pleasure to the suitable bride with whom he eventually settles. As for the older woman—well, she enjoys the same satisfaction that good teachers receive when sharing their wisdom and expertise with apt students.

To what degree, say, the French or Italians still practice this introductory education is not entirely clear. In any event, it's not a tradition that has found much purchase in the far more sexually conservative soil of the United States. Our young men and women tend to learn on each other, at younger and younger ages, though we do provide plenty of prostitutes should a male prefer that more traditional venue.

Whatever you might think of this custom as an educational vehicle for the young, it has a very relevant application for the rest of us—male and female. Because, frankly, the young are not the only ones who have sexual uncertainties. As noted, you probably have a few of your own. And while there are approaches to overcoming these anxieties on your own (diet hard, breathe deep, buy great lingerie, leave the lights off, close your eyes and think of Bloomingdale's . . .), nothing is as effective as a reassuring lover to reawaken a woman's sexual self-confidence. Enter the sexual mentor.

In *Sex and the Seasoned Woman*, Gail Sheehy refers to this man as the "pilot light lover"—a transitional figure who "reignites a midlife woman's capacity for love and sex." Sheehy reports that this figure appears in women's stories of transition, and indeed he does. He might well appear in yours, or—failing that fairy dust—you just might go out and find him.

A sexual mentor is a man with whom you have a positive, perhaps even ongoing, sexual experience. Ideally he is a man who likes women, enjoys sex, and has very little to prove for himself sexually. He is simply focused on sharing the delights of the moment. At best, this man understands that a woman who is returning to the sexual stage after some period of retirement needs a supportive, slow, erotic, reassuring, warm reentry. And it's his pleasure to provide it.

Say, where do you find that particular sexual prince?

You may have found him already, without really recognizing it. Often those palate-cleansing antithesis relationships are sexual mentors in disguise. Because you have been so accustomed to being in a partnership, you may have started out viewing your palate-cleansing boyfriend as couples material, introducing your kids, comparing future plans, and struggling to ignore age and social-class obstacles in the interests of love.

These romances run their course, degenerating into the usual monotony of desultory dinners and discovering each other's flaws. On reflection you might realize that the most important role this man played in your development was to reintroduce you to sex so that you could feel good about it again. That's a gift—even if he did simply stop calling one day, the jerk.

So you might have found a sexual mentor without even trying. On the other hand, you might need to go out and look.

This search does require a certain humorous self-confidence, but what the hell—if you can't walk to the edge at this point in life, when will you? The quest involves identifying likely prospects and then having the fun of approaching a man with this particular sexual agenda in mind. At the very least you will have some amusing conversations.

Perhaps the best-publicized search for her own version of sexual mentor was undertaken by Jane Juska, who famously ran the following ad in the *New York Review of Books*: "Before I turn 67—next March—I would like to have a lot of sex with a man I like . . ." Juska recounts the rather poignant tale of the responses she received in her memoir *A Round-Heeled Woman*. At the very least you might find her experiences instructive.

But it is not in any way necessary to reach out so publicly for a mentor of your own. In fact, a discreetly arranged lunch, a glass of wine, and an appetite for frank discussion can accomplish the same goal. That's what worked for Valerie, whose husband of twenty-two years decided, at long last, to come out as gay. His admission left Valerie, at fifty-eight, divorced and self-aware. She had been willing to ignore her own sexual feelings for the many years it had been since she and her husband had enjoyed an active sex life. "I avoided thinking about it during our marriage," she admitted. "So many of my girlfriends joked about hardly having sex anymore that I just figured we were normal. Being left for a man, though, definitely is not what you'd call normal."

Rather than analyze her sexual inhibitions further, Valerie determined she'd overcome them. But that, in her opinion, required a willing partner. "I'm pretty outspoken, and I think I look good for my age. Okay—I mean not wildly beautiful, but I'm fine. So I picked out a guy and figured I'd go for it."

The guy was a single friend and colleague she'd known for years. "We've had a very mild flirtation going over the years. Really, probably no more than he has with lots of women. He's one of those men who flirts with women because he doesn't know another way to relate. But I liked it, and him, so I thought he might be receptive. In the end, I invited him to lunch and told him, 'I asked you here today because I have a problem and a proposition.'"

Valerie explained that since her recent divorce she was "feeling shy and a little awkward about sex." She said she was "looking for a man who would be willing to show me the ropes" and she wondered if her friend might be interested. "He was way less startled than I expected. It took him about two sentences to grasp what I had in mind, so I guess he's been propositioned before. He just started smiling and took it from there."

Of course, after a six-month affair Valerie did fall a little in love with her mentor, which made for some hurt feelings and a sticky ending. They were not, a year later, still friends. But Valerie had returned to her sexual self and she felt better prepared to turn single. "I did end up wanting more of a relationship with him than was in our original agreement. When he didn't return those feelings, I admit, I didn't take it well. But there's no question that I am more whole than when my marriage ended, and that is all to my good."

Falling in love is one of the risks of enlisting a transitional sexual mentor. Of course, rejection is another. "I decided I wanted a sexual experience, period. At an out-of-town business conference, I thought I saw an opening when I went to dinner with a very friendly colleague. After dinner, when he asked, 'What do you want to do now?' I looked him right in the eye, trying to be sexy, and said, 'I want to do whatever yoooou want to do.' He got right up, saying, 'Well. I've had a long day. See you in the morning.' He didn't even give me a chance to give him the no-strings-attached speech. Pretty humiliating."

Humiliating, yes. But not annihilating. The romantic life involves risk—no way around it. But none of that risk is fatal. You may get your feelings hurt, but you already know you'll recover. You may get rejected, ouch, but you just might not. In any event, you will think better of yourself for reaching, instead of sitting passively by, waiting for life, love, or sexual pleasure to come find you.

Your own first transitional relationship, or the second or third, might fit neatly into one or more of these four categories. Then again, you might recognize only a thread of these common dynamics, because you are busy creating your own version of boyfriend and it doesn't resemble anyone else's operating principles. Or, quite frankly, you might have fallen in love, and then all bets are off.

Intense romantic love does sometimes come and find us, no matter what our age or capacity for reasoning. When it does, if it does, for a while your relationship's dynamic underpinnings won't matter to you. You will pretty much not be able to see straight. Should you find yourself falling in love, well, there's nothing to do but hang on until the acute passion passes and you are returned to yourself.

Falling in love, passionately, wildly in love, is a temporary insanity worthy of both envy and compassion from those observing your irrational acts. Some, like Abigail Trafford, author of *Crazy Time*, even see falling in love as a critical step in the process of healing from divorce. It might well serve the same function for someone healing from the death of a spouse. Falling in love is, in effect, a vehicle for emotional reawakening. You were numbed enduring an unhappy marriage or perhaps shell-shocked by an assault of grief. Falling in love is feeling again—feeling thrill, joy, desire, and hope, along with uncertainty, anxiety, and longing—and with those feelings, you are alive again.

You'll know you are there because your body is suddenly a tuning fork, weird, tense, and straining toward the time you will see him. When you are together time may slow down, if only because you are released from the purgatory of waiting. Your longing for this man creates so much energy that you actually think you could heat your home with it. You are solar-powered. You don't even believe that you used to be tired, because you don't get tired anymore.

You are magnetized to him, in thought as much as in body. One widow, shocked at her sledgehammer of passion when she began dating her investment adviser, explained, "It's the only time in my life that being stuck in traffic was a blessing. I had all the time I wanted to think these same thoughts over and over. 'Remember when he . . . ? How about if we . . . ?' I couldn't get enough of it."

In the compelling grip of that kind of infatuation, you will hardly be interested in analyzing this lover as a caretaker or a palate cleanser or anything else. Instead of analysis, you are simply driven to be with him and surprisingly uninterested in anything that is not him. One woman shared a note slipped under her door from a four-year-old grandchild whose birthday party she had missed in order to take a long delicious car ride with the man she couldn't get enough of. "Nana," the note read, "I miss you and the iguana misses you." It was a sweet note, this nana reported. And she did feel a pang of guilt. But such was the intensity of her desire at that time, she couldn't imagine making a different choice.

Insanely-in-love passes—to our regret and relief. With time, a steady stream of mutual affection and the absence of impossible obstacles (like his wife, or a seriously troubled child, or physical distance), your passion might evolve into a deep, abiding attachment, perhaps in the form of a solid, happy remarriage. On the other hand, it might simply run its course for one or both of you, an infatuation that peters out with familiarity. Or it might end in heartbreaking loss, reopening the wound that sent you back into romantic life in the first place. But, barring such variables as a forced separation (which can make obsession linger indefinitely), your period of being completely in the grip of insane love will be a matter of anywhere from two months to three years.

This overwhelming sensation of the world well lost for love is something we associate with inexperienced teens who are happy to blow off a family obligation in favor of a ride on a boyfriend's motorcycle. It's not something we anticipate at forty or sixty. (In fact, this same nana reported that friends took her to lunch and teased her by pretending to throw her a Sweet Sixteen.) But it does happen, rarely, enviably, at whatever age. When it does, you will go with your desire as best you can, all the while managing to fulfill your adult responsibilities when your heart is elsewhere. The people who love you will feel it, and they will probably protest your absence.

You certainly don't need to be wildly in love for your new relationships to rock your circle of friends and family. In fact, almost any romance, transitional or otherwise, will have an impact on your kids, no matter their age, and on your friends, no matter their right. New boyfriends take up previously occupied space, and we all feel a little awkward moving over to make room. You'll want to be prepared with a strategy for social management.

Block or Tackle

Almost as soon as you have a date, it will occur to you to worry about what to *do* with that date—and not just in the restaurant or at the evening's end. At some point you'll start imagining showing up with that date at your club, your family dinner, or simply on Saturday night with the old friends whose company you and your husband once enjoyed together.

Those friends continue to meet for pasta and a movie on

Saturday evenings. Sometimes you still join them—on and off, when you feel like it, if your friends are openhearted enough to include you. Now it's Saturday night again, and you have this . . . boyfriend. This . . . date. This . . . who knows what or for how long. When, exactly, do you bring him along? And what can you expect when you do?

This is the social version of the far more emotionally intense (but not necessarily more difficult) family introduction of a new man who is sleeping with Mom. We've discussed your kids' fantasies, needs, and expectations at length in chapter 4; we've examined the range of responses your friends might have to your newly single status in chapter 6. Each of those discussions, though, centered on the inward reactions of the people closest to you. Whatever those thoughts or feelings, you still have your own interpersonal dilemma: When and how to mix and match a new man with the established people?

Think block and tackle. Then stop overthinking. Walk the path between those extremes and you'll be fine.

Block. Create a zone of privacy around your romantic forays and maintain it for slightly longer than your friends or family might prefer. They can be a little bit curious; you can be a little bit self-protective. Together you will strike the right balance.

A zone of privacy is not secrecy. A secret is something withheld, is often maintained by a lie, and usually harms close relationships, whether it is discovered or not. But privacy allows you to have some aspects of your life that are personal. You make no secret to your friends or family that such private zones exist; you set those boundaries forthrightly, and you are the one to decide when it is appropriate to alter them.

In terms of dating, secrecy means that you hide a date, pretend to others that it did not occur, and perhaps make up a lie to account for your absence. Frankly, sometimes such secrecy is necessary. If, for example, you are going away for a weekend and you don't want your kids (or even your elderly parents, should they still be inquiring) to know that you are sleeping with a new boyfriend, you may have to fabricate a convenient seminar or an out-of-town college reunion to cover your tracks. It happens, and occasionally it's best.

But don't make a habit of it. By and large, secrets and lies are leaky boats. The secret sneaks out, and your relationships with important people sink to new lows. It's preferable to simply stake out your right to privacy and hold your ground. Privacy means that you acknowledge to your friends that you have a romance going, but you intend to keep that relationship to yourself for a while.

Tell your kids, when (and only when) they ask, that you are dating and you will introduce them to any man who becomes important to you. Otherwise they don't need to be a part of your romantic life, unless you feel they will make a constructive contribution. You might tell your friends the same thing, though usually you'll want to tell your close girlfriends every random detail of an encounter because the telling is half the fun of dating. (Sometimes it's most of the fun.)

Whatever you tell friends or family initially, a point will come when you might include a new man in your familiar world. When? How? How much? This brings us to tackle.

Tackle. Take on the reactions of your social network to a new man. A successful tackle involves four steps:

- Timing your introduction.
- Preparing the ground briefly.
- Smiling your way through the meeting.
- Keeping the postmortems to a minimum.

Timing is a function of your own comfort level, your personal values, and, to a degree, outside circumstances. In the end, though, *it won't be perfect and it doesn't have to be.*

With respect to family, some newly single women take the position that they are adults with a right to a romantic life and their adult children should recognize and respect that right. Besides, they don't like to sleep alone.

That woman brings a lover home at the outset of the relationship. If a child happens to be sleeping in the same house, well, so be it. Even if she maintains the fiction that the relationship is not sexual—by insisting that the new man leave the house very early in the morning, for example, or that he spend the balance of the night in the guest room—the kids understand the situation. Frankly, they don't like it.

Kids (and we could be talking here about kids of forty) struggle to accept a sexually and romantically active mommy. They can get to that peaceful acceptance, but it's a journey with plenty of mother-child bumps along the way. Your overall goal is to protect your relationship with your kids while satisfying your own needs for romance and intimacy.

You'll probably do that best by including a new partner cautiously, and only when the relationship seems to have emotional importance in your life. If you are having a post-divorce, promiscuous, hookups-for-happiness period, best to schedule that for the weekends when you are alone in the house. That might make the long Christmas break, when your college-age kids descend on you, a bit of a lonely sexual spell, but it's a wise trade-off. And you've endured lonely sexual spells before, right? Hey—you were married.

In the end, though, who is to say exactly when a relationship merits an introduction? That timing is more about your heart and your sense of your family than it is about the length of time in the relationship. As one woman said, "I was divorced for nine years before I let a man sleep in my house. But the man I finally invited over was one I'd known for only a month. We fell in love, boom. And my kids, who do live with me, are all in their late teens now. I decided it was time to let them see this side of me, because I wanted to include this man in their lives from the beginning. The kids were shocked. But we've all gotten through it."

You'll surely get through it too, but it's best to treat the introduction of a new romance to your kids as a meaningful thing that requires a deliberate decision, rather than as a casual event that merits no conversation. Once you do decide, though, *don't overthink it, and don't overprepare.*

Keep the emotional drama to a minimum. "Jack is coming over for dinner Sunday. He's a man I've been dating for a while." Period. You might answer a few basic questions—"Who is he, Mom? What does he do? How did you meet? Are you going to marry him?"—but keep it light, and tell them they'll have a chance to form their own impressions.

Then smile through the dinner and don't make too much of how anyone reacts. Don't look for instant warmth and friendship on either side. As long as the family is civil, as they would certainly be to any guest, don't press further. It takes some time to get used to seeing someone sit in Dad's chair—even if they don't particularly like Dad, even if Dad's chair has been empty for longer than he ever occupied it.

Envision this process as a case of the emotional hare and tortoise. You probably have the anxious hare's hope that your children and your boyfriend will experience that instant click of friendship that transforms all of you into an immediate happy group. But it's the emotional tortoise that usually wins this race. Breathe deep and allow all parties to go at their own emotional pace. Trust that, over time, each will find something to like in the other. Or not.

As noted in chapter 4, adult children bring their own fantasies to your romantic relationships. One seventy-year-old woman, who remarried last year after twenty-three years of being single, described her kids as initially being "a bit disappointed" with her choice. "I think they wanted me to marry a WASP icon—you know, a silver-haired retired banker with whom my sons could sail and golf. My new husband is anything but that. Neither was their father, but I think that's the kind of dad they always wanted. My new husband is very quiet, far from Mr. Dynamic, and my boys just couldn't see the attraction. I could, though, and I told them they don't have to love him, they just have to be polite. They are, and now he's won them over."

You too may have to allow that period of time to adjust perceptions and thaw defenses. These openings of the heart occur best outside the spotlight, so discipline yourself to avoid asking for immediate feedback. "So what did you think?" is a natural inquiry after you present a new man to an old friend or to an adult daughter. But that question asks your daughter or friend to commit herself openly to an assessment. It's harder for her to soften that assessment later.

If a friend or family member offers up a postmortem (whether "Gee, he seemed nice" or "Mom, have you lost your mind?"), resist delving too deeply. You don't want to carve any of these first impressions in stone, even the good ones.

Be prepared for your adult children to fall into the role of protective parents once they are included in your romantic life. These attitudes can range from the absurdly judgmental ("I'm just not sure he's good enough, smart enough, ambitious enough for my little mom") to the comically cautious ("Can he drive a car at his age? In the snow?"). You cope with these kindly intended but irritatingly patronizing interventions by turning them lightly aside. ("Thanks, darling, I love you too" will suffice.)

Tackling the integration of a new boyfriend with old friends is also tricky, though in a different way. Timing will be determined through some balance of your social needs and your personal anxiety. On the one hand, you want to bring a date to the dinner party; you are tired of being the fifth wheel on Saturday nights. On the other, you hold back. You hate to admit it, but you are worried about being judged.

You fear the group's verdict. How does this new man stack up against your former partner? How well does he fit into your social group? Not that you care so terribly what your friends might think. But still . . . your ex was a jock, a total guy's guy, and so are the other husbands with whom you socialize. How will they connect with this date who is far more interested in NPR than the NFL? Your deceased husband was worldly, a wine connoisseur and traveler. Your boyfriend is something of a cowboy, unconcerned with proper silverware and unprepared for social chitchat. You can see yourself in bed with him, but you just can't see him at the dinner party.

To a degree, your friends are simply a projection screen for your own concerns about this new relationship. What works privately, on a trip or in an embrace, does not always translate into the other corners of your life. An evening with friends opens your relationship to more than the reactions of those friends. It opens it to your own critical judgment, and you might not want to face up to that quite yet.

When you do decide to risk it, whether through the pressure of outside circumstances or your own deliberate decision that it's time, follow the same three cautious steps recommended for family introductions. Prepare the ground briefly, by saying you are coming with Jack, a man you've been seeing. (If you've already ruined this step by telling your friends every affectionate comment Jack has ever made to you, plus his whole financial situation since the divorce—oh well. Keep moving.)

Smile through the evening, and don't try so hard to get quiet Jack to talk more, to get geeky Jack to wear the right jacket, or to get show-off Jack to shut up and make a better impression. You are too old for any of these hopeless renovation efforts anyway. Just relax, let Jack be Jack, and see how you feel at the end of the evening. Or the month.

Try to minimize the morning-after reviews, too. Give your friends a chance to get comfortable with Jack. Over time they may surprise you with their flexibility, or they may turn out to be every bit as narrow and judgmental as you always knew them to be. Doesn't matter, you love them anyway. And you are too old to start dropping old friends just because they have character flaws.

You are not, however, too old for love. It's not clear yet what form that love will take, or with how much of your life it will overlap. Your Jack might be suitable only for a private corner, and that might end up being just fine with you. Or you might realize that he is a transition to another fuller, more realistically based relationship.

You are in process, trying things on, testing yourself, using friends, family, and sometimes a stranger at the gym as sounding boards for your evolving version of love this time around. As it crystallizes, so it will be more likely to come to you.

After all, seek, and ye shall find—right?

CHAPTER NINE

Grail

We shall not cease from exploration
And the end of all our exploring
Will be to arrive where we started
And know the place for the first time.

—T. S. Eliot
Four Quartets, "Little Gidding," V

Where does all this starting over end you up? Closer to love? To God? Closer to your children or your own truest self? Closer to the brass ring of happiness, maybe even so near that you could reach out and grasp on for a moment as you ride by?

Could be.

Could be that you end up with some or even all of these

riches, though probably not, say, all on the same Saturday. However much of what you seek you actually find, one thing is certain: You will be in very good company.

Millions of men and women turn single at life's midpoint and beyond. Certainly not all, but very many wish to resume some variety of romantic life, given the opportunity and the ability to minimize its costs.

They seek soul mates or bridge partners, travel companions or dinnertime conversation. They seek the social cover of an escort or the physical comfort of a warm body in an otherwise empty bed.

Some newly single women are planning the flowers for the next wedding long before they've met the groom. Others are perfectly content to wallow in please-myself solitude and sprinkle romance over their days like chocolate into coffee—an added spice, but not a necessary one. As you well know, these might both be the same woman—maybe even you—when considering the question of love on different days.

Men in their infinite variety reapproach romantic life according to their different needs as well. One views his life in partnership, and replaces his loss as soon as possible. Another has a job opening for full-time resident female and he keeps that position filled. Period. A third shares only his Saturday nights and his sexual needs with whichever attractive and willing partner might suit him at the moment. And everything in between.

Each of these people has experienced a loss, and each of them has moved toward starting over in his or her fashion. Like you. So where does all this starting over end up?

It might end up with a new and deep and enduring love

or with a great friendship. Or both, if you have a lot of love to offer and luck is on your side. It might end up with your spirit mending from your loss, stronger where the tear was, reinforced by some support or attention or bottomless affection whose source you do not know today. You found it because you started over.

We both know that there is no guarantee that it will end up well. You could experience another divorce, though thankfully not as horrific as the last. But still wounding, and at a time in life when it takes longer for every injury to heal.

You could end up alone, no tragedy except to those who fear it. But many of us do fear it, and fear that's where we will end up. It's a possibility that should not be denied. Nor, frankly, should it be dwelled on. Only know that you increase the likelihood of that outcome if you sit on the side and hope life will come to your rescue. Pray to God but row to shore.

You could resume romantic life convinced that just the occasional flash of male—the rare dinner, the out-of-town tumble, the office flirtation—is more than enough seasoning to carry you through your days. And then at a bus stop you get into a conversation and now you have a seventy-three-year-old boyfriend and his grown children are hostile because they think you want Dad's money and your own daughter is miffed because you don't want to babysit as often anymore and your quiet life is suddenly full of complicated emotional drama. Is it worth it?

Sure.

It's worth it because it puts you in the full center of the messiness of life, and that is a fine and interesting place to be. Worth it because the view from this center at fifty or sixty is so different from what life looked like thirty years ago. You are getting a chance to view love and relationships and romance from the perspective of your long experience. You have arrived back where you started, but surely you are seeing this place for the very first time.

Resume romantic life, yes, but then discover that the ensuing experience is not entirely under your control. (And how many times have you had to learn that bitter lesson over the years? Well, here it is again.) Sometimes you put your toe in the water and the tide unexpectedly sweeps you away. You will flounder for a time, naturally. But don't be afraid. You're a grown-up now. You can swim.

Still, it must be said that, whatever rewards you are seeking and whichever in the end come your way, the game can be costly. The purpose of this book has been, in part, to reduce your emotional price and to make your efforts more successful.

Continuing in that vein, those interviewed for this book have offered you the benefit of their advice and experience. Take this free advice for what it's worth, know that it has been heavily edited, but do consider its wisdom on its merits. In resuming your romantic life, as in so many other aspects of living, there is much to be learned from those who have gone before.

Advice from the Front

You'll probably find plenty on this list that you already know, and just as much with which you may disagree. But you could also learn something, or at the very least, remind yourself of something you've known but forgotten to adhere to. Think of these as the ten commandments of romantic reentry. Surely you'll break all these directives at some time. Still, especially when you are just starting out, romantic life works better when you follow these rules.

1. Solidify your female friendships. You need your long-standing girlfriends, and you must make room for and invest time in new ones too. They are anchor, base, life support. From that base, you can take a great many risks. Without them—you've given yourself no parachute.

2. Just say yes. Simple, obvious, and powerful. Open yourself to every opportunity short of premature sexual intimacy. When you say no, you have any number of valid reasons. In the end though, that leaves you stuck with your reasons. Reasons are cold comfort.

3. Take your time. A relationship driven at hyperspeed by your own anxious need to connect is a heartbreak waiting to happen.

First, it takes time, maybe a really, really long time, to know yourself and what you want. Take the time to find out, or you'll end up in a relationship with whoever comes along. Those don't work out so well.

Second, it takes time and practice to learn to take care of yourself. The better care you can take of yourself, the less needy you will be with a partner. The less needy you are with a partner, the more apt you are to get a good one.

Third, only time on the job can help you to distinguish a completely legit guy from a bullshitter. In those heady, early relationship days, frankly, the two look and sound alike. There is no tea leaf reading substitute for getting to know someone, impatient though you may be to figure out where this is going.

Finally, women afraid of being alone often connect with men fearful of making another mistake. The urgent press for more relationship panics Mr. Fearful, and he's apt to flee. Take your time, for both your sakes.

Barring a dirty bomb or a dreadful diagnosis, you have the time to let a relationship unfold, so your head has a chance to keep pace with your heart. Take that time and use it to your advantage.

4. Appreciate the fragility of men. Understand that everyone who comes into your life has his own broken pieces. Repair takes its time, and, though you may long for it, there is no quick fix. Or rescue.

In particular (but not exclusively), a man coming out of a divorce may feel humiliated, have an ugly sense of failure, or be especially guarded. Since the only socially acceptable image for a single man is hot and ready to roll, women often mistake this projected image for his interior reality. Sometimes, of course, it is. How to tell the difference? See commandment number 3.

5. Do not complain. Not as a joke, not as a witty story, not in a heartfelt, self-revelatory moment. Keep your problems—especially your miserable ex, your depressed kid, your financial mess—to yourself, until the man in whom you are confiding actually cares about you and your life. This may well take twice as long as you think it should. Follow this commandment anyway.

Certainly, you are feeling brittle, vulnerable, afraid, even overwhelmed. It's normal—you're new at this. Bring it to a therapist, not to a new relationship.

6. Pay sane attention to your body. What you look like matters.

You do not need to be ruthlessly self-critical. You definitely do not need to starve or surgically Barbie-your-body into big boobs and a whittled waist (unless this is your own idea of a good time). But—romantic life is served best by a body in reasonably good physical shape. You do need the gym. You do need to give up soda, smoking, and sweets—most of the time. You will miss them. Oh well.

7. Risk. Nobody is going to come knocking on your door. And *pity me* is not an attractive place to be. If you are lonely or sad . . . do something, call someone, join something, go somewhere.

8. Walk and talk with confidence. Practice until you are able to enter a party alone, sit at a decent bar alone, go out to dinner alone. Once you can, take the risk of smiling at a stranger and responding should he choose to approach. It's grown-up play, once you get the hang of it.

9. Be sexually open (but not so open that your brains fall out). Set a sexual standard that feels right for you. Maybe he has to buy you a drink, maybe he has to know your middle name, maybe he has to be a candidate for marriage. Whatever that standard, uphold it with humor and self-assurance. You are a consenting, experienced adult and you can set your own sexual rules for right and wrong. Just make sure you live by them.

If and when you do become intimate, take the risk of letting your lover know what you want and need. Many women who talk frankly about politics, art, or even anger will not tell a man what they want in bed. Those same women, thoughtful and attentive lovers themselves, are unwilling or unable to be open about their own pleasure. Men, especially more mature lovers, long to know. Tell them.

10. "The better is the enemy of the good." Don't let the critical, perfectionist, entitled voice in your head drown out your joy. It surely will, unless you fight it off.

Nearly everyone interviewed expressed some variation on this point, from "Have realistic expectations" to "Don't wish for so much from men in the beginning" to "There is no man who will fix your life."

The most trenchant version of this advice was offered by an experienced and much-pursued bachelor: "The two big problems in relationships are that women are never satisfied, and men choose not to pay attention."

Give yourself the biggest break—be willing to be satisfied. It's a secret to happiness. Maybe it's even *the* secret, come to think of it.

The Happy Part

The path to happiness and the cure for back pain actually have a great deal in common. Experts are eager to guide us with confidence in many a concentric circle.

Happiness, we are advised, must be found from within, except that it depends on your relationships with others. Happiness is best discovered when you are not seeking it, except that it helps to identify your life's purpose and therefore know what you are looking for. Happiness, it's said, is all about the journey, but you can't have much of a journey if you don't know where the hell you are going.

(By the way, back pain can be cured by exercise, except when it can't. It responds well to rest, unless rest makes it worse. Or you might try the surgery, which will be a catastrophic mistake unless it works, in which case you will wonder what took you so long.)

Happiness is the Grail. Your life carves the path. Time is your capital. How to spend it, especially these days when you have a more acute sense that you are spending capital that will not, cannot, renew? How to invest what's left wisely? How to maximize your shot at that Grail along the way?

It is fashionable, even mandatory now, to continue to seek a high level of satisfaction in this second half of life. We are urged to reinvent ourselves, to reinvigorate our lives with new purpose. We are exhorted to flee our empty nests, to find new meaning, press on in our spiritual journeys, and to do it all with bodies we can push to new limits if we lavish them with love and exercise, blueberries and broccoli.

No need to pack it in, we are assured. It could be better than ever now—different, yes; not young, never that again. But something maybe even better than young. A life force tempered by wisdom, benefiting from experience with the vision and health and energy to give back, do good, climb mountains, and kiss strangers.

And we are responding by the legion, zipping off to African orphanages, counting the highest peaks in our neighborhood and hauling ourselves up them, then giving speeches that celebrate these accomplishments. Bush senior threw himself out of a plane and Miz Lillian was ahead of her time trooping off to the Peace Corps in her seventies. Now tens of thousands follow in her wake—volunteering across the globe or in our neighborhoods, solving the climate change crisis or the problem of the missing traffic light a block away that has resulted in far too many accidents.

We are back at school, back on our bikes, and back backpacking—all returns to the joys of childhood savored even more after years of adult responsibility. We are back at work too, starting companies because we love to test our skills against the marketplace, or getting ourselves hired in strange positions because we need the money.

And we are not through with romantic love either, even if it does sometimes appear to be a higher mountain than most. Who knows how far along the romantic path the game will take us at any one time? But many of us have decided to take the chance and play.

In all these ways and so many more, we have become the students of Dylan Thomas, who commanded us, "Do not go gentle into that good night." We are listening and we will not and we are not.

But maybe Dylan Thomas was wrong. Maybe all the second-half-of-life enthusiasts are wrong or overstate their case. At least there is a legitimate alternative point of view.

Perhaps the wisest way to greet that good night we are all facing is gently, calmly, and with a full acceptance that the time has come. It could be that you decide at some point to sit comfortably on the sidelines and simply watch the circus as it parades by. It could be that you are happiest there, that that is where you find your Grail.

However you decide to greet the night, I hope you have a chance to do it holding hands.

AUTHOR'S NOTE

This book is largely addressed to women, because women are the customary readers of its type. But if you are a man who is resuming romantic life, you too will likely be awkward and emotionally raw. If you've found your way to this book, I think you will find that it applies to you as much as to the life of the woman you next look over, over coffee.

And this book mostly refers to the tribulations and successes of heterosexuals who reengage in the pursuit of love. Gays and lesbians also experience brutal breakups or the devastating death of a partner—left alone and without even the social structure of legal divorce or formal widowhood to ease the passage to the next life phase. This book does not include an evenhanded discussion of the similarities and differences of these experiences, because I didn't do a thorough-enough study to speak with authority on them.

But male or female, gay or straight, we all reel after the loss of love. Then every one of us has the daunting, complex, and exhilarating task of re-creating it. And there's no way around it. That new love requires getting naked again.

SOURCES

The information in *Getting Naked Again* is based on my thirty-five years of clinical and social experience and observation. In addition, over the course of two years I conducted some one hundred interviews with single men and women from their late forties to their early eighties, each of whom had returned to the dating life relatively recently. Some were widowed, some divorced, some out of long-term dating relationships, and a few had been through all three of these experiences and were in a position to make comparisons.

These interviews did not constitute a quantitative scientific sampling. (The best scientific surveys of this population that I know of have been done by AARP, should you be interested.) Instead I conducted a series of confidential conversations with willing subjects who were introduced to me by colleagues and friends. I simply asked everyone I knew if they might recommend me to recently single adults, over the age of fifty, whom they considered smart or thoughtful.

Fifty was an arbitrary age, and in fact, in the end I included the thoughts of people in their midforties as well. The idea was only that a woman newly single at thirty-two would seem to encounter a different set of issues than would that same woman at sixty. I was more interested in addressing those later concerns and so confined my interviews to that age group.

The interviews were meant to be a qualitative investigation designed to confirm, reformulate, or expand the impressions I had formed through my years of clinical observation. During these confidential interviews, I did use a standard set of questions as a jumping-off point, though I tended to try to follow where the conversations led. These interviews took place across ten states, on the phone, in person, and sometimes through follow-up e-mail. They varied in lengths from perhaps half an hour to several hours, depending on my sense of the comfort level of the participant and the productivity of the conversation.

The synthesis of this qualitative interview material with my clinical and social observation is entirely my own, subject to my own biases and distortions and my own relentless, irritating optimism. I believe in love. I am convinced of the possibility of love. I am committed to supporting the growth and development of love—at whatever time in life you seek it, and wherever you or I might find it. Love, I believe, is the point, and that's why I wrote this book.

Judith Sills, PhD
Philadelphia

ABOUT THE AUTHOR

Judith Sills, PhD, is a clinical psychologist, a three-year National Science Foundation fellow, and the author of five other psychology books that have been translated into eleven languages, including the bestselling *Excess Baggage: Getting out of Your Own Way, A Fine Romance: The Passage of Courtship from Meeting to Marriage,* and *The Comfort Trap; or, What If You're Riding a Dead Horse?* She is also a former radio host and nationally recognized public speaker and writer. Her work has been cited in the *Washington Post,* the *New York Times, USA Today,* and the *Chicago Tribune,* and she has contributed to most major women's magazines, including *O, The Oprah Magazine; Redbook; Mademoiselle;* and *Cosmopolitan.* She is a Juvenile Diabetes Foundation Super Achiever award winner, and a Books for a Better Life finalist. She has a Philadelphia-based private practice in clinical psychology.